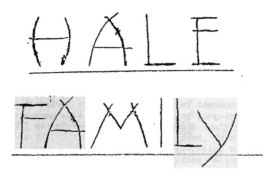

# HALE FAMILY

\*\*\*\*\*\*\*\*\*\*\*\*\*\*\*\*\*\*\*\*\*\*\*\*\*\*\*\*\*\*\*\*\*\*\*\*\*\*\*\*

The Hale family is one of the oldest families in the territory
now included in the bounds of Tennessee. Several brothers migrated
from Virginia ( Bedford and Lunenburg Counties) to the Watauga
settlement as early as 1778 and there became the founders of that
State, which by it's patriotism has long since gained the name of
"The Volunteer State". The oldest deed in the records in Tennessee
(then North Carolina) was witnessed by one of these brothers. The
Baptist Church in Tennessee was begun through the efforts of these
Hale brothers, Nicholas, Heshack, Shadrack, Abednego and probably
others. A brother-in-law, Rev. Matthew Talbot was among them.

The notes in this collection are, of course, not all that can
be found on the Hale family in Tennessee, but do largely give de-
tailed information on this family's entrance into the territory
of Tennessee. From this settlement and as time passed, scarcely
a County in the State, by the year 1850, was not lacking in some
way a connection with this family.

\*\*\*\*\*\*\*\*\*\*\*\*\*\*\*\*\*\*\*\*\*\*\*\*\*\*\*\*\*\*\*\*\*\*\*\*\*\*

Research made and compiled

by

Mrs. Edythe R. Whitley
Historian & Genealogist
2710-Belmont Blouvard
Nashville, Tenn.

1934

Nicholas Haile ( Heale) of York County, planter, who in 1654, gave a power of attorney to Dr. Thomas Roots in Lancaster Co. He is suceeded in the record by George Heale, who executed a power of attorney, November 8, 1677, and whose wife is named, as Ellen in 1682.

George Heale ( Nicholas) was sworn justice of Lancaster Court in 1684, and in 1695 and 1697 he served as a member of House of Burgesses. He names in his will Dec. 30- 1697 and proved in Lancaster County Jan'y 12-1698, son-in-law, Mr. William Ball and issue: Nicholas, George, John, Joseph, Ellen. His widow Mrs. Ellen Heale, made her will October 15, 1710 which was proved in Lancaster County, Dec. 13- 1710. She names issue in addition: Elizabeth, Sarah, William, Hannah, wife of Capt. William Hall. According to a Division of her estate Jan.5- 1710, daughter Ellen Heale, married Opie, probably John Opie who married secondly Ann Metcalf and was father of Lindsay Opie.

George Heale (Nicholas) will December 3, 1697 proved Lancaster County Jany 12- 1697-98. His wife will dated Oct.15-1710 proved Lancaster Co. Dec. 3- 1710 according to these he had. Hannah married William Ball, George, John, Joseph, Nicholas, Ellen, Elizabeth married Wm Davenport Nov. 26, 1728, Sarah married 1715 Newman Brockenborough, William born after the making of his fathers will.

George (George, Nicholas) married Catherine Chinn daughter of John Chinn. George Heale made his will proved Sept. 23, 1736:

Issue: Ellen born Nov. 19-1705 .    Elizabeth born March 8- 1710, Catherine, Sarah, William married Judith Swann, 1734.

( Willian & Mary Quarterly,Vol. 17 pages 202, 203, 204, 297)

****************
William Heale son of George son of Nicholas of Lancaster Co. Virginia had a son George ( oldest child) born 8 Sept.1728 died 1808.
( Tyler's Quarterly, Vol. 7 page 286).                    2016539
****************

Ann Heale married Dec. 20- 1736 Moore Fauntleroy.
Betty Heale married July 9- 1749 Kendall Lee.
Wm. Fox in his will 1747 names Elizabeth daughter of Capt. Geo. Heale as a legatee.
Joseph Heale vestryman Lancaster Co. 1739.
John Heale, of Lancaster County dec'd will dated Nov. 29-1739 gave his nephew George Heale of Lancaster , Gent., 1830 acres of land.
George Hale Justice of Richmond County Virginia 1706.
George Hale sheriff Lancaster Co. 1724-5.
John and Joseph Hale, Justice Lancaster 1734. ( in most cases in all these notes name spelled Heale).
(Hayden's Virginia Genealogies. page 55.).
****************
Virginia Land Patents and Grants on file in Richmond Virginia in State land office. are to be found a number of references of Heale, Hail, Hale, Haile.

Francis Heale and Wm. Heaberd 1300 acres, between Petomecke and Rappa Rivers nigh branches of Pasbytansee Creek extending to land surveyed for Wm. and John Heaberd, crossing the Doiggs path , crossing branches of Rappa. River 9 Feb. 1663. For the transportation of 26 persons including Joyce Hales, Fra. Hailes,

Recd O 8 8-1978

1.

James Hailes.

Martin Coale, 400 acres Northumberland County Oct. 5- 1653. Abutting Sly upon Wicocomico River. Ely upon land of George Heale, Transportation of 8 persons.

Coll William Claybourne, Sect'y of State 750 acres Northumberland County 14 June 1653. Abutting Sly upon the soverail plantations of Martine Cole, George Heale.

Mr. Nicholas Heale ( written Nathaniel and erased) 738 acres Lancaster County Virginia 18 May 1666. Upon North West branch of Corrotoman River upon the North east side beginning at the mouth of a small cove which runs up to the sai Heale house and c. Being one-halfe of land granted to Enoch Hawker and Anthon Doney ( or Dowory) 29 July 1652 conteyning 1000 acres and sould to said Heale by said Howker, see that more land being contoyned within the bounds of said pattent then the pattent expresseth, the residue above the one moyety thereof being 238 acres in due said Heale for transportation of 5 persons: Jno. Jancy, Mary Wms, Ann Hubberd, James Hawley and Will Miles.

Capt. Francis Morgan and Ralph Green 500 acres Glocter County 13 Jan. 1652 for transportation of 16 persons including Nicho Heale.

Nicholas Heale 500 acres Lancaster County June 1- 1657 upon the northeast side of the northwest branch of Corotoman River opposite plantation of Henry Davis Being one-half of patent granted to Enoch Hawker 29 July 1652 and purchased by said Heale. Renewed 9 Feb. 1663.

Capt William .Tucker Esqr., and one of the Councell of State of Virginia 100 acres at the back river within the precincts of Elizabeth Citty or at withi the mouth of the broad creek 1 June 1633. for transportation of Richard Heale and William Elberry whoo come in the Eleanor 1622.

Other immigrants found in the Land records are : Simson Heale, Symon Heale, Wm. Heale.

Marke Johnson 198 acres in Eliz. Citty Co. July 31, 1645. transportation of 4 persons includihg Nicholas Haylo.

William Bodlam 70 acres 29 Nov.1652 Commonly known by the name of Yeocomoco Point. Bounded with a Creek which divides this and land of Thomas Hayle.

Barbara Hayles transported by John Rookwood Gent., before Aug. 20- 1651.

There is an Edward Hale mentioned as early as 1635. Thomas Hale in Elizz City County Virginia as early as 1636.

********************
Edward Hale ( 1750-1820)married Patsy Perdue and had Mary Hale ( 1805-1881) married 1825 Jno. B. Williams. This Edward Hale served in 1781 at Guilford Court House and Witzell's Mill. In 1782 he served in expedition against the Indians. He was born in Virginia and died in Franklin Co. Virginia. (D.A.R. Lineage Books. Vol. 107 page 279).
********************
Caleb Hail, Auditor's Accounts of Revolutionary War. Va. State Library.
William Hail ( Westmoreland) Rev. Army. Va. State Library.
Caleb Hale ( 13 Va. Reg.). Va. State Library. Richmond. Virginia.

Edward Hale served in 3rd Virginia Regiment in the Revolution. Va. State Library.
John Hale served 9th Va. Regiment in Revolutionary War, Va. State Library.
Thomas Hale served in 4th Virginia Regiment in the Revolution. Va. State Library.
William Hale ( Augusta Co. ) Revolutionary Army.   Va. State Library.

*******************

### Some   Hale Marriages in Virginia

Franklin County, Virginia.

Jane Hale to Joshua Barton, surety, Thomas Hale , Jan. 11-1800.
Susannah Hail, daughter of Stephen married Wm. Camp. Dec. 4- 1790.
Mary Hale daughter of Wm. Hale married Wm. Campbell Feb. 25, 1789.
Elizabeth Hale to John Craghead, April 3- 1786.
Sarah Hale to Solomon Grimmett , Sept. 18, 1794.
Armstrong Hale and Elizabeth Ruble daughter of Owen Ruble, Jan. 10-
1789.
Benjamine Hale Jr. and Dicey Frankling, Benjamine Hale Sr. Surety.
Nov. 13, 1783.
James Hale and Jenny Craghead daughter of John Craghead Oct. 2-1786.
James Lewis Hale and Ann Crahead daughter of John Crahead, July 20-
1789.
John Hale and Susannah Wade daughter of John Wade , March 17-1789.
John Hale and Doshea Saunders Sept. 12-1792.
Joseph Hale and Sally Turnbull, July 20-1789.
Joseph Hale and Eliz Turman  Feb. 13- 1789.
Maxey Hale and Dicey Crahead  Oct, 25. 1789.
Peter Hale and Sarah Morris, daughter of Zekel Morris, Surety
March 14- 1791
Richard Hale and Tibatha Jones Oct. 24- 1788.
Wm Hatcher and Patty Hale, James Edmundson Hale , . Surety. Aug. 8-
1796.
Robert Hodges and Susannah Hale daughter of Isham Hale, May 18-1791
Daniel Hough and Hannah Hale daughter of John, born Aug. 30- 1790.
Jesse Jones and Hannah Hale daughter of John Hale , Sept. 2- 1788.
David Mattox and Sally Hail, Dec. 1- 1806.
Rachel Hale daughtor of Joseph Oct. 23-1789 to Thos. Porter.
Sarah Hale to James Vier, Thos. Hale Surety. Nov. 4- 1803.
Rachel Hale daughter of Benjamine to Josias Vier. Jan.2- 1800.


Grayson County Virginia Marriages:

Polly Hail and James Atkins Oct. 31- 1822.
Polly Hail and James Brewer  June 11-.1822.
Sarah Hail and Joseph Bryant, May 1824.
Absolom Hale (Hail) and Mary McCloud, Apr. 4- 1822.
Preston Hale and Elizabeth Comary (Conoy(?)) Oct. 17, 1816.
Rufus Hale and Nancy Hail Aug. 16- 1835.
Stephen Hale and Charlotte Dickerson, Aug. 4- 1814.
Stephenand Hale and Rosamond Bourne, Jan. 9- 1834.
Thos Hale and Sally Sutherland July 4- 1817,
W. B. Hale and Matilda Jones Jan. 31- 1833.
Wicks Hale and Peggy Bryant, June 6. 1822.
Lucenda Hail and Zra (Ezra) Nuckolls. Apr. 10- 1823.
Polly Hail and Minetrea Pool. Nov. 13- 1823.
Keziah M. Hale and Russell Rogers. Mar. 7- 1836.
Seaby Hale and Wm. Rutherford, Feb. 12- 1822.

3

Meshack Hail married Catherine Gibson daughter of James Gibson in Bedford County Virginia before 1763. ( see will of James Gibson of Bedford Co

**************************

King George County Virginia ---- Cyprian Anderson to Susannah Anderson, his widow, ---- Edward Hoyle, sec. f. Feb. 1744, ii 424.

***********************

SOME REVOIUTIONARY SOLCIERS OF VIRGINIA
All found in Virginia State Library at Richmond.

Edward Hail
Leonard Haile (Hale) Nelson County.
Samuel Hail
Thomas Hail ( Henry Co. Militia).
Thomas C. Hail
Wheeler Hail
William Hail
Caleb Haild.
Samuel Haile
William Hale ( Hanover Co. ).
William Hale ( Richmond Co. ).

Caleb Harl ( War 4.p 214)
Caleb Hall ( Bounty Warrant.).

William Hale was pensioned from Richmond County Virginia  Oct. 20- 1819 aged 73 years. He served as a private in the Virginia line. ( U.S. Pensions

Leonard Hale received from Nelson County Virginia a pension. He served as private in Virginia Militia. Pensioned March 26- 1833 then aged 78 years. ( U.S. Pension Records , Washington D.C.)

Thomas Hale served in Revolution from  South Carolina but received a pension while living in Franklin County Virginia.  Pensioned Feb. 1- 1819 aged 77 years  dropped May 1- 1820 , Reenstated Jan. 28- 1831.  ( U.S. Pension records, Washington D. C. ).

Anthony Hail received a pension 1825 while living in Perry Co. Ky. for his services in Virginia line in Revolution. In 1825 he was 82 years old (U.S. Pensions).

Isham Talbot received Pension in Bourbon Co. Ky. 1818 for his Revolutionary service in Virginia. He was 75 years of age in 1823. (related to Hale Family.)( U.S. Pension records)

*********************
Nucholls History of Grayson County Virginia has a great amount of Hale family history, including picture of Arms.
********************

Rev. Matthew Talbot ( 1729-1812) died in Wilkes Co. Ga. married Mary Haile (1728-1785) ( Virkus , Compendium of American Genealogy Vol.5. page 339).

********************
George Heale 1728-1808 of Fauquier Co. Va.  was Burgess, married Sarah Smith. ( Virkus, Compendium of Amer. Gen. Volume 4. page  372. )

4

Meshack Haile. ( Hennings Vol. 7. page 205). 1758 September. To the
Militia of the County of Bedford and Provisions furnished by sundry Inhabitants
of the said County, etc. etc. "To Gross Scruggs and Meshack Haile, sergeant
---- 7 £ . 5 s. 4 d. each."

*************

John Pratt and Polly Hail married in Bedford County Virginia
Sept. 7- 1792.
William Banister ( widower) and Ann Haile (widow) married Bedford
County Virginia, April 26- 1763. Isham Talbot surety.
Robert Woodcock and Ann Haile July 6- 1793 · consent of Stephen and
Nancy Haile, the parents of Anne. Bedford County Virginia.
Laban Haile and Molley Haile. Oct. 7- 1799. married consent of
Stephen Haile guardian for Molley. Bedford County. Va.
William Moody and Sally Haile married Feb. 18- 1792 consent of
Stephen and Nancy Haile parents of Sally. Bedford Co. Va.
Charles Dabney and Betsy Hale married March 26- 1798. Henry Davis
surety. Consent of John Hale father of Betsy. Bedford Co. Va.
Thomas Haile and Jenny Moodey married Feb. 10- 1793. Bedford Co. Va.
William Haile and Suckey Maxey, married Oct. 24- 1796. Bedford Co.
Virginia.
Meade Hale and Betsey Jackson, married March 7- 1796. Bedford County
Virginia.
Jonah Hale and Elizabeth Howell, married Oct. 21- 1795. Bedford Co.

*************

Lewis Hale took oath of Allegiance in Henry County Virginia and Thomas Haile
was Captain of Company in same County in 1781. ( History of Henry Co. Va. by Hill
pages 307 and 233).

*******************

John Haile, Henrico County Virginia Nov. 8- 1770. John Hailes Gent.
John Haile Gent. May 4- 1771 Henrico Co. Va. ( Justices of Peace of Colonial
Virginia by McIlwaine. page 137 and 108).

*******************

First List of Tithables of Pittsylvania County Virginia for year 1767
Cambden Parish ---- List of John Donelson 1767 --- Joseph Hale. ( Hist. of
Pittsylvania Co. Va. by Clement , page 276).

*******************

Meshack Haile. H. S. 7-205. This means Hennings Vol. 7. page 205.
( Report of the State Library of Virginia. List of Colonial Soldiers of Va.
page 44.).

*******************

Census of 1790 shows Lewis Haile in  Essex County Virginia.
Shows other Hales in this same county .

*******************

Crozier's Virginia Colonial Militia. Bedford Co. Sept. 1758.
Matt Talbot and Charles Talbot.   Shows Sergeant Meshack Haile. ( page 67)
John Hailes in Brunswick Co. Sept. 1758 as private ( page 70). Shows Edward
Hale in Thomas Burke Co. May. 30- 1774 in Lord Dunmore's War 1774. ( page 79).
Militia of Surry County 1687 shows Nathaniel Hales. ( page 102).

5

The marriage of John Hales in Henrico and Elizabeth Miller of the parish 1760 Feb. 20. ( Douglas Parish Register. Goochland Co. Va, by W. Mac. Jones. 1928).

Will Hales and Susanna Payne in Goochland 1771 June 26. ( same reference).

1797 will in Goochland County Virginia of William Hale.( same ref).

*************** *

James Rees born May 26- 1770 died 1863 and married Nancy Hale born Feb. 12- 1772. Died August 9, 1853 native of Virginia, settled in Lincoln Co. Tenn.  ( Reliques of Rives by Childs. page 269, pub. 1929).

****************

In Loudon County Virginia ---- John Hale married Maria Craine. Hale died and she married Edwin C. Brown. George Hale was his brother.  (Va. Soldiers 1776 by Burgess. Vol. 3. ).

*************

Hales Ford is in Franklin County Virginia.

*********** *

Susannah Hail of Virginia ( born 1766 daughter of Benjamine. Capt. American Revolution married Kate Ferguson) married ᴗᴗ(his first wife)1788 James Blakeney ( born 1765).  ( Abridged Compendium of American Genealogy Vol. 2. pag' 271. better known as Virkus).

*************

William Brown came from England or Scotland about 1632. His son or grandson William lived in Prince William Co. Virginia and married a Miss Hales, daughter of John Hales. The will of John Hales, dated 1727 Westmoreland Co. Va., devises land in Stafford Co. Virginia to his grandson William Brown and to his so George Hales and Daughter Mary King.  ( Genealogy of the Brown Family of Prince William County Virginia, by James Edgar Brown, 1930. page 18.  see also page 54

****************

Torrence in his wills of Virginia gives the following: Joseph Hail, 1785 Inventory, Albemarle Co.; Richard Hale ( Hail) 1784 will. Bedford Co; Jno. Hail, 1814 will, Isle of Wight Co.; Edward Hail  will 1757. Isle of Wight Co.; Elizabeth Hail. 1757 will. Isle of Wight Co; Benjamine Hail 1794 will, Sussex County; Francis Haile, Bedford County, 1780 will; Jane Haile 1782 Inventory Bedford Co; Jonathan Haile, 1737 will, Essex Co; Jno. Haile,1744 will, Essex Co. Mary Haile, 1753 will, Essex Co.; Jno. Haile, 1761 will. Essex Co; Edward Haile will 1756 Essex Co.; Richard Thomas Haile, will 1795 Essex County; Jno. Haile of Isle of Wight Co. will 1794; Hannah Haile 1799 will Isle of Wight Co; Jno Haile 1774 inventory in Pittsylvania Co; Benjamine Haile 1799 will in Sussex Co; Pool Hale, Inv. 1728 Isle of Wight Co; William Hale, 1762 Inventory, Isle of Wight Co; Edward Hale, 1676 will, Surry County; Charles Hale 1677 will York Co; Thomas Hales, 1658 will. Northumberland County; and Jno. Hales 1728 will in Westmoreland County. Virginia.

6

LUNENBURG COUNTY VIRGINIA RECORDS:

A list of tithables from the mouth of Falling River upwards for the year 1748
-----Taken by John Phelps--- Nicholas Hail with 4 Tithables.

The same for 1752 ---- List taken by John Phelps --- Mrs. Nicholas Hail,
Shadrack Hail with 5 tithes and Nicholas Hail Junr, eith 2 tithes.

At June Court 1749 the appointment to take the list of tithables were made as
follows:
Nicholas Hayle (Haile) from Goose Creek to the extent of the County upward.

List of tithes taken by Nicholas Haile 1749. Nicholas Haile with 4 tithes.

In 1750 List taken by Nicholas Haile shows him with 3 tithes.

List taken by Nicholas Haile 1749 shows Nicholas Haile Junr with 3 tithes.

List taken by Lyddall Bacon 1752 shows John Hale.

List taken by Wm. Coldwell 1752 shows ( assisted by William Haills list) James
Millword with 2 tithes.

****************

Cumberland Parish Register, by Landon C. Bell. page 291. says Matthew Talbot
married Mary Day. She was probably a young widow whose maiden name was Hale.
(She died 1785.) Matthew Talbot and Mary Hale had a son Edmund Talbert born in
Bedford County Virginia March 28, 1767. (There were other children also.).

***************

Some Deputy Sheriffs of Gloucester County Virginia 1787 ---- William  Hail
Junr, and Robert Yates. ( Virginia Historical Magazine, Vol. Jan'y 1934 page
65).

******************

Lewis Hale is mentioned in Virginia Historical and Biographical Magazine
Vo. 9 page 139.

****************

In the 1932 pension list of Tennessee. Bledsoe County, John Hale aged 80
years in 1831 pensioned. He served in the Virginia line during the Revolution.

****************

BEDFORD COUNTY VIRGINIA RECORDS:

Fee Books ----1778, Richard Haile, page 23, May 1778  Rec. Murpheys deed to
you.-------100

Fee Book --- Meshack Haile, page 109. 1778, Meshack Haile ( guase whether
not Abednego) Dr. # Tobo. . ---- Sept. cont. vs  Smith   15.

Fee Book.---- John Hail. 1773  page 170. Dr. ---May, Rec. Overstreets deed to
you.-----1.00. Augt. atto ads Woodward 5 Impl. 15 Sept. Plu. 10.---30

7

Fee Book.--- 1773. Meshack Haile. page 210. --- Octr. Meshack Haile. Dr. --- Decl in Eject to Threetout Watts, 5 Dock. 5 ---- 20. ---- Nov. cont. to Threestout 15 ------.

Fee Book. 1772. Feb. Lewis Haile. page 12. ( 9 entries of cases pertaining to him )

Fee Book. 1770. Abednego Haile. page 43. ---- ( several entries in his name)

Fee Book.--- 1770. Jno. Haile. page 69. --- ( 2 entries in which a Qusenberr is mentioned.).

Fee Book. 1774-5-6-7- John Haile page 179 ( many cases of John Haile).

Fee Book 1754-1761 no Hales, Hailes mentioned.

1767-- Fee Book ---- Jno. Hail page 12.-- Jany Cont. to Baber 15/Feby) Tryal to Jud. 10 Tax 177.--- Co. to 11 Co: & Co: 21 int. to Wil All. 40 copies 40.

Fee Book.--- Page 7. Jno. Haile. --- Dr. ---- Jany Pet & Sum ---- Echols 50 atto 5 --- Jud ---- 55. ---- Exson v Echols 23 ( Feby) the same 23 ---46. --- Feby Pet° & Sum.----- Farmer 50 atto 5 ---- 55.

Fee Book.--- 1769. Mr. Abednego Haile ---- Dr. ---- Page 16.--- Jany Exom v Brooks 23 (Feby) the same --- 23 ----46.--- Feby Atto ads Hook & co. 5 Imps 15-- 20.--- Sepr.-- Exom V Brooks. 23 (Octr) the same 23---46.

Fee Book. 1765 Dr. Luke Haile. page 77. --- Dr. Lbs Tobo. Aygt. Endor add you to List of Tithables 15 copy 10..25.-----

Fee Book --- 1766 Jno. Haile. page 20. June pet & sun.----- Walker 50 atto. 5 Cont. 15.----- 70. ----- Boil ret. to Baber to Ord. 15. -------25. -----July Order v Baber 15 ------- 15. ---- Aug. Order v Baber 15 Joinder 10 ----- 25. Sepr. Ordr. over Rule Decr. 15 V. Eng. 10 -------25. ---- Ordr take Depr. of Wilson v Baber 15 Dedinus 25 ------ 40. ---- 1 Sur (?) v Baber --- 10 ----. Nov. Cont. v Baber 15.

Fee Book 1764 no hale, Haile, -+- etc.

Fee Book --- 1768 Abednego Haile , page 29. ---- Dr. Feby Peto & Sum v Brooks 50 atto 5 Ord. 15. N. Pro. 10 --- 80. ---- Mar. Ord. v Brooks 15 a. Sum 10 ----- 25. --- July Exon v Brooks & c. 23 Aug the same 23 (sept) the same 23..... 69. ----- Augr atto Ads, Hidson 5 Impl. 15 -----20. ------- Pleas adv. Hidson 10. ----- Nov. Exon v Brooks 23 the same in Oct. 23. the same in Dec. 23.----- 69.

A deed in Book K. page 374. 1801. Laban Hail from Jno. Allen & etc.

### Bedford County Wills.

Francis Haile, will. Proved Aug. 1780. wife Adara: ch. Richard, Stephen, Lewis, Elizabeth, Mary, Ruth, Usholy, and Mourning. Will Book A. 1. page 376.

Inventory of Francis Hail same reference. Sept. 27. returned to court 23 Oct. 1790.

In the will of Guy Smith , probated Sept. 1781 wife Anne, daughter Elizabeth Smith, daughter Anne Trigg, daughter Joanna Hail. Bird B, Guy, Lucy, Susanna, Kate Bowker, Jenny.

Inventory of Jane Hale deceased. April Court 1781. Will Book A-1. page 425.

Will Book. A-1 page 462. Will of Richard Haile. recites himself of Bedford County. Wife Elizabeth Hail, children: Sarah Hatcher, John Hail, Elizabeth Hail, James Hail, Martha Hail, Richard Hail, Frank Hail, Powel Hail, Molly Hail, Lewis H il, ------ Some of these children under age. Wife Elizabeth Hail, executrix, Stephen Haile, my son John Hail, and Humphrey Edmundson executors. dated 19th Nov. 1783. witnessed Richard Demondson, John Hail, Humphrey Edmundson, and John Smith. Proved June 28- 1784.

Deed Book #.E-5.---page 327.---- John Haile and wife Ann to Jno. Burden all of said county. Aug. 20- 1775. Land Jno. Haile purchased of Overstreet.

Deed Book D-4 page 151. Indenture made 6th day of April 1771 between Peter Finnie of the one part and Meshee Haile of the other part. Consideration of 50 pounds current money. Tract of land containing 200 acres in Bedford County:Beginning at white oak on southside of Falling Creek thence of north eighty eight degrees west ninety six poles to a post oak, south fortyfive degrees west, one hundred and ten poles to white oak in patent line off cross line , north twenty six degrees was one hundred and fifty poles to Hickory north forty five degrees East eighty poles to patent corner pointers thence on patent line north seventy five degrees east fifty six poles to Hickory south sixty three degrees east one hundred and ninety six poles to Falling Creek and thence up the said creek as it meanders to the first station with all woods waters ways and all other profits commodities. etc. Witnessed by Wm. Mead, Bo$^d$ Gaines, Simmonds Everett. signed by Peter Finney.

Dedford Co. Deed Book D-4 page 390. Deed 23rd September 1772 between Meshack Haile of one part and William Mead of the other. For consideration of 100 pounds to him in hand paid the receipt whereof is hereby acknowledged sells to William Mead tract of land 200 acres. This is land on Falling Creek being same as purchased by Meshack Hail from Peter Finny. Catherine wife of Meshack Hail acknowledges the sale. Sept. 28- 1772.

Order Book. 1754-1761 May 27- 1754 the first entry of the County of Bedford. No Hail entries, on first page. Page 8. Mark Cole, Thomas Morgin and Wm. Morgin to view the Road from Nicholas Hail to Thoms Wright and make the Rept & c. ---- July 1754.

Deed Book C-3.page 176. March 11- 1768 Nicholas Hayle of Baltimore County Province of Maryland to William Heath of Bedford County Virginia. for 20 pounds current money of Virginia--- pd. by Heath to Hayle for 400 acres lying in Bedford Co. Va. on both sides of Lenwells Creek. Nicholas signs but his wife does not. Witnessed by John Talbot, John Quarles, and Robert Baber.

Page 180 same book dated 168 a bond pertaining to the same deed as above.

Book of Deeds A-1. --- Page 159.--- Deed. Plantation and house whereon I now live and the land on which the improvements is made and as I have not got my potent for the same I do appoint and constitute my Loving friend William Mead as lawful atterney to act and do as if I myself were present and in name to make William Rentfro a right according to law to the said land, containing 300 acres

signed Nicholas Haile and Ruth Haile. witnessed by Jerem Yarbrough, James Yarbrough and Hanna Yarbrough. Proved in court 27th March 1758.

9

Deed Book A-I. page 160. July 27- 1757 between Nicholas Haile and wife of Rhan County North Carolina to Wm. Renfro of Bedford Co. Colony of Va. 350 acres of land in Bedford Co. Va. lying and being on the Waggon Road called Rentfroos Road and on a branch called Indian Run in Bedford County. Signed Nicholas Haile and Ruth Haile.

Will Book. A-1, page 20. Will of James Gibson of said County. Dated April 14- 1764 proved Feb'y 26, 1765 mentions : son James Gibson, Randall Gibson, daughter Elizabeth Chandler, dau. Catherine Hale, daughter Hanner Cook, son-in-law Joseph Gibson. son John Gibson deceased heirs ----. heirs of my son Archbell Gibson, dec Test Jerh Early, Henarrete Bosel, John Wainright.

***************

GRAYSON COUNTY VIRGINIA WILLS.

. Dudley Hail will. proved Feb. 1815. names wife --- Nancy, children Preston, Burris, Lewis, Polly, Franklin, Sally, Jesten, Olive, and Elizabeth.

John Hail deceased assignment of dower to wife Rosemond Jan. 1850 Heirs -- Thomas, James D Warenr, John , William, Stephen, Loranza D, Johnson, and Sidney Hail.

Lewis Hail deceased appraisement returned April 1802.

William Hail will probated May 1847. names wife Lucy; children Peyton, Susannah Bryant, Rosamond Dickerson, Elizabeth Whitman, Stephen, Charles, Samuel M. sons-in-law Morgan Bryant, John Dhickerson and David Whitman. The children of his sons Lewis and John Hail and the child of his daughter Nancy Gose, the children of his daughter Susannah Bryant. The children of daughter Elizabeth Whitman and children of daughter Rosemond Dickerson.

******************

VIRGINIA CENSUS OF 1790 HALES

Hail, Benja. found in Sussex County Virginia.
"     Benjamine, found in Sussex County.
"     Edward , found in Nansemond County Virginia.
"     Jno. found in Sussex County.
"      "      "     " Nansemond County.
"     Micajah, found in Sussex County.
"     Thomas found in Isle of Wight County.
"     William, found in Richmond County.
Haile, John , found Isle of Wight Co.
: "      "      found in Essex County.
"     Lewis, found in Essex County.
"     R. Thomas, found in Essex County,
"     Wheeler, found in Essex County.
Hale, Anne, found in Northumberland County.
"     Daniel found in Hampshire County
"     Edward , found in Nansemond County
"     John, found in Northumberland County.
"     John, found in Nansemond County
"     John, found in Northumberland County.
"     Samuel, in Nansemond County
"     Thomas in Mecklenburg County.

10

# SOME  MARYLAND NOTES IN HALE FAMILY

****

The General Assembly of Maryland  passed an Act 1742 in accordance with the
the petition of rector and vestry of St. Paul's empowering etc. --- Nicholas
Haile to receive voluntary subscriptions for buying a piece of land and building
a Chapel on it. Soldier's Delight Hundred.--- ( Maryland Historical Magazine
Vol.1. page 149. 1906. ).

***************

Will of John Kellan Senr. of Somerset County, Maryland March 2- 1739 proved
21 May 1744 mentions a daughter among other children Anne Hale.

Baltimore County Maryland. 27th Feb. 1729-30 proved Apr.18-1730, To eldest
son Nicholas and heirs ½ of "Haile's Fellowship", where he now lives; son
George to have upper end next to George Hitchcock's; said sons dying without
issue,"their portions to pass to heirs at law. To wife Frances, extx, dwell,
plan.  Part of Merryman's Lott" and  Heils Addition", eldest daughter Mary (for
division see will). and personalty. ^ Daughter Hannah and Daughter Ann.  Daughter Millisant and daughter Sabbiner, son George.

**************

Nicholas Hale son of a Nicholas Hale moved to Baltimore Maryland from Roan
County North Carolina. He had moved from Bedford County Virginia to North
Carolina. He left Baltimore Maryland and moved to the Watauga Settlement N.C.
(later Tennessee) ( see pension record of his sons and will wills under Tennessee
records).

***************
------------------------------
***************

## SOME GEORGIA NOTES IN THE NAME HALE.
*****

Elbert County Georgia.  Alex Vaughn and Elizabeth David married Aug. 20- 1807
by Isaiah Hailes.
  Matthew Talbot when a young man married a young widow ( with one child, a
dayghter) by the name Day, her maiden name being Hale and they had six children,
One record in print says Matthew Talbot married Mrs. Mary Hale nee Dale.

. John Stewart's son Rouben went to Clark Co. Ga. and married Charity Hale.

  Silas Hales was a private in Benton's Regiment in 1782.

  Joseph Habersham Collection of Georgia. Vol.2. page 84. says--- Lewis Hales
1795 appraised estate of David  Dawson.

Many Hailes and Hailes in Georgia very early, during and after the Revolution.

  Historical Collections D.A.R. Vol.2. 1902. page 54. Georgia. Rev. Matthew
Talbor died 1785 married Mrs. Day ( nee Haile) had Rev. Edmund born 1767,
Charles, William, Matthew Lewis died 1776, Thomas Green, and Haile. Dr. James
Talbot married Miss Haile.

11

Wilkes County Georgia.

James Hale married Polly Jackson, Nov. 1- 1820.
Joshua Hale purchased property at sale of Wm.Kelly April 1791.
Nathaniel Hail and Nancy Ogletree married June 8- 1811.
William Hail paid poll at John Muligans in 1802.
Benjamine Hale asked that a clear title be given to land on Oconee River in
Baldwin County, by Felix Hay and Richard H. Long executors of Gilbert Hay, deceas
John Hale draws land Lottery in 1806.
Joshua Hale draws land lottery 1803.

\*\*\*\*\*\* \*\*\*\*\*\*\*\*\*\*\*\*\*\*\*\*\*\*\*\*\*\*\*\*\*\*

-----------------------------------------------

SOME NOTES FROM KENTUCKY RECORDS ON FILE

Montgonery County.Kentucky.

Francis Peyton will. Book B. page 213-4. 1810 proved 1816 names Elizabeth
Hale as a daughter.

Daviess County Marriages.
Jane hale to David Brown, Aug. 22- 1818.

Mercer County Kentucky.
Ann Hale ( Book 1 page 195) widow of Joseph dec'd settlement of estate. To
school and board 3 children. Adnrs. Thos Freeman and James Hanna and Joseph
Willis. Recorded Oct. 1794.

Jobe Hale ( Book 1 page 109) names wife Hannah. Eldest son Isaac, son Johnny
when sons are of age. 3 daughters Betsy, Nancy and Sally. Recorded and proved
1793.

Joseph Hale dec'd Inventory 1793.

Will Book. 2. page 74. Names wife and infant children, Exec. Jesse Hale.
March 9- 1798 prove 1798.

Philip Burris will names Mary Hale wife of Thomas Hale. 1854.

Garrard County Kentucky.
Abraham Hale and Martha Fitzgerald married Oct. 11- 1798.
Lincoln County Ky. marriage Samuel Rennich and Ruth Hale April 1- 1796.

:   In Mercer County Thomas Hale married Elizabeth Deaine, June 22- 1802.
    In Mercer County John Days and Nancy Hale married April 11- 1805.
    In Mercer County Nathan Stein and Sally Hale married April 16- 1807.
    Mercer County Ky. John Hale and Sarah Barnett dec. 8- 1808 married.
    Mercer County, Betsy Hale and Daniel Dooney married Aug. 16- 1810.
    Mercer County, Casandra Hale and David Devine married Jan. 19-1815.
    Mercer  County, Betsy Hale and William Long married Aug. 2- 1815.
    Mercer County William Hale and Sally Borders married March 5- 1818.
    Mercer County, John Hale and Louisana Ledgers married April 2- 1821.
    Mercer County, Elias Hale and Polly Plue married July 15- 1824.
    Mercer County, Samuel Hale and Eliz. Mee married Feb. 9- 1826.
    Mercer County, John Hale and Catherine Dorothy Rice, married May 18- 1826.

Mercer County, Jesse Hale and Mary Stagg married July 22- 1830.

At Pisgah Church in Woodford and Fayette Counties. Sept. 3- 1053 Joseph Hale received as a member.

In Lexington Kentucky among the early graves: Garland B. Hale born 2/11/1809, died Nov. 14- 1893.

\*\*\*\*\*\*\*\*\*\*\*\*\*\*\*\*\*\*\*\*\*\*\*\*\*\*\*\*\*\*\*\*\*\*\*\*\*\*

--------------------------------------------------------

## SOME NORTH CAROLINA RECORDS OF THE HALE HALE

( Records pertaining to that section of North Carolina
which later was Tennessee not included in this section but
included in the notes from Tennessee.).

North Carolina Historical Commission, Raleigh, N.C.

North Carolina Revolutionary Army accounts. Vol.1. page 58 folio 4.
An account of Specie Certificates paid into the Comptrollers
office by John Armstrong Entry Taker for Lands in North
Carolina Vizt.

| No. | By whom granted | To whom Granted | Date | Sum |
|---|---|---|---|---|
| 3435. | Williams Carter | Shadrack Hail | 12 June 1783 | £ 10. 4. 0 |

| Interest | To what time | Total Amo. Principal & Interest. |
|---|---|---|
| 0. 4. 6 | 28 October 1783 | £ 10. 8.6. |

Same reference page 51 ---- folio 2. is found:

| No. | By whom granted | To whom Granted | Date | Sum |
|---|---|---|---|---|
| 70 | Williams & Carter | Shadrack Hail | 19 June 1782 | £ 17.2.0. |

| Interest | To what time | Total Amo. Principal & Interest |
|---|---|---|
| £ 1.7.0. | 28 October 1783 | £ 18. 9. 0. |

Same reference. Vol. 1.page 69. folio. 2.
An account of Specie Certificates paid into the Comptrollers Office
by John Armstrong Entry Taker for Land in North Carolina vizt.

| No. | By whom Granted | To whom Granted | Date | Sum |
|---|---|---|---|---|
| 3834 | Bledsoe & Williams | Shadrack Hail | 12 June 83 | £ 10. 4. 0 |

| Interest | To what Time | Total amount principal & Interest |
|---|---|---|
| £ 0. 9. 2 | 16 March 1784 | £ 10. 13. 2 |

Accounts of Comptroller's Office   War of Revolution Book J. page 221.
Issued Certificates for Service performed against the Chicamoga Indians dated
May 24- 1790.
1232  Shadrack Haile for services performed against the Chicamoga Indians  £ 5.17.-

Office of Secretary of State, Raleigh, N.C.  Land Grants ---- Shadrack Hail 200
acres Nov.10- 1784  entered June 18- 1781 Washington Co. ( not a military grant).

13

NORTH CAROLINA WILLS:

Edgecombe County North Carolina -- Benjamine Haile, witness to will of
John Marshall. ----1757.

Edgecombe County North Carolina, will of Thomas  Smith 1757. Benj. Haile,
executor.

Albemarle County North Carolina. Hanna Haile witnessed will of Richard Elks.
in 1687.

Bertie County N.C. 1732. John Hailes was one of the legatees mentioned in the
will of Thomas Pollack.

Chowan County N.C. --- 1741. Elizabeth Hale ( 30 pounds bill money of this
provience) in will of William Trigg.

Chowan Precinct. N.C.--- 1710. John Hale witnessed will of Isaac Hill.

William Hale mentioned as uncle in will of William Flovell, at Newton
County not given and says. late of Nassau in New Providence. Dec. 1737.

Chowan County. N.C. --- 1738 In the will of Henry Bonner is a mention of
Hale's plantation.

Halifax County, N.C. 1797 Aris Hail mentions in his will --- Sarah (wife), and
Nancy.

Halifax County N.C.--- 1797.  Robert Hail, in his will mentions William,
Judith and Samuel also a Thomas.

Rowan County N.C.---- 1766 John Halo, will mentions Ann and Arminda.

******************

CENSUS OF 1790 FOR NORTH CAROLINA:

Hail, Aris. Halifax County.
  " , Dudley, Warren County.
  " , Jesse, Halifax County.
  " , John , Stokes County.
  " , Jonathan, Halifax County.
  " , Lewis, Halifax County.
  " , Ogburn, Halifax County.
  " , Williamson, Halifax County.
Haild, Jacob, Randolph County.
Hailo, John. Dobbs County
Hailer, Henry, Johnston County.
Hailes, Chapman, Johnston County
Hailes, John, Johnston County
Hailes, John Senr, Johnston County
Hailes, Robert, Robeson County
Hails, John, Edgecombe County
Hails, Mary, Rowan County.
Halo, David, New Hanover County
Hale, Foroby, Hertford County
  "  , Jesseo, Bertie County
  "  , John, Bertie County
  "  , Jonas, Bertie County.

Halo, Matthew, New Hanover County
  "  , Nathan, Bladen County
  "  , Polly, Nash County
  "  , John, Edgecombe County
  "  , Josiah, Chatham County
Hayles, Daniel, Cumberland County
  "  , Hosey, Cumberland County
  "  , James, Cumberland County
  "  , James, Northampton County
  "  , Joe, Cumberland County
  "  , Jonas, Northampton County
  "  , Joseph, Robeson County
  "  , Joshua, Sampson County

14

Revolutionary Soldiers in North Carolina by the name Hale ( not a complete list).

Isaiah Hales, private N.C. Militia ( see his pension Hickman Co. Tenn.).

William Hale, private N.C. Line. ( see McMinn County Tenn.).

Chapman Hayles, private. pensioned from Johnson County North Carolina. He served in N.C. Militia. Pensioned in 1832. In 1831 was 73 years old.

Joseph Haile, private pensioned for Rev. service while living in Lancaster District South Carolina under Act of 1818. He served in North Carolina Cont'l line. Pension began Jan. 13- 1831 when he was 77 years od ago. He died July 13- 1832.

### SOME NOTES ON THE HALE, HAIL FAMILY FROM MISSOURI

******

Benjamine Haile, pensioned in St.Genevieve County Missouri after having served in the Missouri rangers. Pensioned March 5, 1817.

*********************

Lilburn Hale, born March 14, 1815 in Sullivan County Tennessee son of Lewis Hale, born 1794 and his wife Elizabeth Bragg ( daughter of David Bragg). Lewis Hale was son of Meshack Hale of Greene and Washington Counties Tennessee. Meshack's wife was Mary Kincheloe. Meshack was son of Shadrack Hale and Mary his wife of Washington County Tennessee, and Bedford County Virginia. ( Lunenburg County Virginia). Lilburn Hale married in Sullivan County Tenn Dec. 24-1835 Sarah Clark, born Mar. 8- 1813 (daughter of James and Frances Clark of Sullivan County and Washington County Tennessee.) died Nov. 24- 1892. Lilburn Hale and wife moved from Washington County Tennessee to Shelby County Missouri about 1843. Lilburn served in the Civil War and was killed in 1862 April 2. His daughter Nancy Ann Hale born in Tennessee Dec. 9- 1843 married Joseph Ridge ( Joseph Richard Ridge) Nov. 22- 1858 died 1902. He was a son of Isaac Ridge of Hickman County Kentucky. ( see Tennessee records).

### A NOTE FROM ILLINOIS RECORDS ON THE HALES

Pension list of Illinois -- Invalid pensioners Sangamon County. William Haile private in the Revolutionary Army. Pensioned Nov. 19- 1811 under law of July 5- 1812.

William Haile, same place and probably same man. Revolutionary Army. Pensioned April 1816. Killed by Indians in 1832.

# TENNESSEE NOTES IN THE HALE FAMILY ----

( Gives as nearly as possible by counties. In some places
remarks will be given from the compiler of this note
book, showing relationship, in most cases are only
notes from records. When remarks by compiler the initials
E.R.W. will follow the remarks.)


## WASHINGTON COUNTY ----

The first deed registered in Washington County was one from Jesse
Walton of State of Georgia to James Taylor of State of South Carolina conveying
200 acres " lying in Washington County, in State of Franklin", May 2- 1785.---
Valentine Sevier and Nicholas Hall ( Hale) were witnesses.

Among the members of the Congress of 1776 were John Haile, Jon
Carter, Charles Robertson, John Sevier. Washington Dist. Watauga Settlement.
( Ramsey's Annals of Tenn. page 139.).

Jonathan Matthew, Isham Hale, Archibald Cowan, Elijah Huzzey,
James Simpson, Edmund Castub, obtained permits to remove property and c. with
part of their families --- April 23- 1798. (This is a Pass Port to enter Indian
Lands ---E.R.W.) ( Land Office. Legislative Papers Boo. 1. ).

Petition from inhabitants of Blount County ( was part of Washington
at one time E.R.W.) asking that a land office be opened for the purpose of
entering the land south of the French Broad between the Rivers of Tennessee and
Big Pigeon 1798.--- among the signers are¹ Luke Hail, John Hail, William Hail.
( Legislative Papers Box. 1.  State Land Office at Nashville, Tenn.).

Thomas Haile, was Ensign in Washington County 31 July 1799 and Lot Scott as
Lieutenant of County Muster which was signed by Zachariah McCubbin, Jesse Hunt
and Thomas Ford. ( Legislative Papers Box. 2. Land office Nashville.).

Petition of John Haile to General Assembly of North Carolina,
for the annexation of the Watauga Settlement. ( Vol.10 page 708-11 of North
Carolina State and Colonial Records).

State of North Carolina Grant No. 287 . 50 shillings for each 100
acres .-- to Nicholas Hail, 300 acres in Washington County, on Sinking Creek.
Oct. 24- 1782. ( N.C. Grants  and deeds to Individuals in Watauga Purchase
page 266  , Tennessee Land Office, Nashville.).

N. C. Grant No. 284, 50 shillings for 100 acres. Nicholas Hail.
640 acres. Washington County. on Sinking Creek. Oct. 24- 1782. ( N.C. Grants
and deeds to individuals in Watauga Purchase. page 271, Land Office Nashville
Tennessee.).

N. C. Grants No. 182. 50 shillings for every 100 acres. Meshack
Hail 348 acres in Washington Co. on north side of Watauga River Oct. 24- 1782
( Land office Nashville. deeds and etc. Watauga Purchase page 289. )

North Carolina Grants Surveyors Grants. in Tenn. State Land Office
at Nashville, ---- Meshack Hail, locator. Grant No. 182.  24 Oct. 1782.---
Meshack Hail ( Hale) Grantee. 358 acres Washington County.

16

Shadrack Hale, N. C. Grant # 739. Aug.10- 1787. Granted Shadrack Hail, 300 acres. Washington County. ( North Carolina Grants on file Tennessee Land Office. Nashville. Book 4, page 425. ).

Shadrack Hale, Grant No. 694. Nov. 10-1784. Shadrack Hail 100 acres Washington County. ( N.C. Grants, Tenn. State Land Office, Nashville. Book. 4. page 426).

Abednego Hail, Grant No 911 Nov. 17- 1790 for 200 acres, Washington County ( N. C. Grants in Tenn. State Land Office. Nashville. Book 4 page 701).

North Carolina Entries found in the Tennessee Land Office, Nashville --------
Abednego Hail. No. 296. Washington County, August 4- 1778. 100 acres for Abednego Hail on a branch above John Carricks the Island Road. Same entered to Peter McNamee and transferred to Hail by order of McNamee. Aug. 17- 1792.

Shadrack Hale No. 510. Washington County. Oct. 17- 1778. on North fork of Limestone fork of Lick Creek including head spring of said fork. 25 March 1779 300 acres. Same surveyed for Shadrack Hale, Jany 24- 1782.

Shadrack Hale. No. 720 . Dec. 21- 1778 Washington County . 100 acres on Lick Creek place called Long Hollow, a branch of Clear Lick Creek. Sept. 14- 1781, surveyed Jan. 24- 1782.

Shadrack Hale No. 2872, for Shadrack Hale. Washington County, June 18- 1781 on Lick Creek and Kendricks Creek, near walnut Valley, Sept. 6- 1782. Surveyed for Hale May 27- 1783.

Meshack Hail, N.C Entry. No. 767. Washington Co. Dec. 24- 1778, for 500 acres at mouth of Lick Creek on north side of Watauga River adjoining John Moores land. Given May 2- 1779. Surveyed for Meshack Hail June 8- 1779.

Philis Hail No.720. Same land granted to Shadrack Hale. 1779.

Meshack Hail. No. 1418. N.C. Entries. Washington County. May 5- 1779. 200 acres of land. on both sides of Lick Creek adjoining a late survey made by said Hail running up the Creek for compliment --- Given 23 Sept. 1781. 100 acres surveyed for Meshack Hail. Sept. 11- 1783. Surveyed again 1792 for Joseph Hipinstate.

*******************************

Shadrack Haile signs Petition ---- Petition of the Inhabitants of the Western Country. To the Honourable the General Assembly of North Carolina now sitting--
The Inhabitants of the Western Country Humbly Sheweth --- That it is with sincere concern we lament the unhappy dispute that have long subsisted between us, and our Brethren on the Eastern side of the Mountains, respecting the Erecting a new Government, We beg leave to represent to your Honourable body, that from Acts passed in June 1784, ceding to Congress your Western Territory with the reservations and conditions therein contained. Also from a clause in your Wise and Mild constitution, setting forth that there might be a State, or States, erected in the west whenever your Legislature should give consent for the same, and from our local situation numberless advantages, bountifully given to us by nature, to propagate and promote a Government with us. Being influenced by your Acts and constitution and at the same time considering that ti is our un.--
deniable right to obtain for ourselves and posterity a proportionable and adequate share of the blessings, rights, privileges, and Immunities allotted with the rest of mankind, etc. etc. ( among the long list of signatures are found) Shadrack Haile. Shadrack Hale, Jr. ( his mark X). ( N.C. State & Colonial Records Vol. 22. page 705-12.).

Albert E. Hale is son of Enoch, grandson of Meshack Hale and Mary Kincheloe
and lives near Johnson City, Tenn. at Austin Springs. (E.R.W.).

Albert Hale's mother was Mary Whitlock daughter of J.T. Whitlock and Elizabeth
McCrary. The widow Elizabeth McCrary Whitlock married as his second wife and her
second husband Lewis Hale.   Lewis Hale's first wife was Elizabeth Bragg. daughter
of David Bragg of Sullivan County Tenn.  Will Whitlock Hale son of Lewis Hale
and his second wife. Mary Whitlock the daughter of J. T. and wife married Enoch
Hale son of Lewis Hale by his first wife. This makes Lewis Hale's step-dau-
ghter also his daughter-in-law. Will W. Hale is living and is the son of a
War of 1812 soldier. Elizabeth McCrary was born 1802 and died 1888 buried at
Austin Springs, Washington County, Tennessee.   Albert Hale has a brother
John Hale who lives at Poor's Knob, Wilkes Co. N.C.  Enoch Hale was in the Indian
Wars ( information from Albert Hale). Will Whitlock Hale was born in 1867. Elijah
Hale a brother of Lewis & Enoch Hale was a doctor and went to Texas.
Charles Hale another brother lived in either Akron or Detroit.   James and David
were brothers. ( This information from Albert Hale). (E.R.W.).

Lewis Hale served in War of 1812 as a private in Capt. James Landen's Company
Col. Sam Bayless' Regiment (4th) East Tenn. Militia from Nov. 13-1814 to Mary
18-1815. ( War Department, Washington, D.C.).   Richard Hale was in the same
company. He married Mary Cox.

In 1842 the list of members of Boones Creek Church in Washington County
included several Hales also as early as 1834. They are : John Hale, ( dec);
Chinowth Hale; Elizabeth Hale; Nancy Hale; _____; Sarah Hale; _____
Sabrina Hale; and Susanna Hale.

Bible Records of E.D. Hale and wife Deborah Massongill of near Johnson City,
Tennessee. Copied from the bible while in their home by E.R.W._____
Fuller P. Hale's Bible.   Fuller P. Hale. Jany 23- 1824. ---- Virginia E. Hale
born Feb. 17- 1853 ---Gentry Hale born Sept. 1-1855 -- Susan Emma Hale born
March 8, 1859 -- Charley Hale born Oct. 6, 1861 -- Elbert Dewit Hale, botn Feby
20-1863 --Jimmy J. Hale, born Oct. 12, 1865 --- Rhoda Glen Hale, born Jan. 19,
1870 -- Walter Burson Hale, born Jan. 29-1874 --- Mary L. Hynds born Feb.
13, 1868(a niece of this family) --- Joseph Fuller Hale born Jan. 8- 1901 ----
Emma Sue Hale, born Jany 12-1903 ---.
Deaths---- Mark Hale died April 6, 1880 --- Charlie M. Hale died Nov. 12-1861 --
Walter Burson Hale died March 1, 1874 --- Orlena B. Hale died March 24, 1874 ---
Jennie E. Smith, died July 17, 1890 --- James J. Hale, died March 19,1898 ---
Carmilita Hale, died June 13, 1898 ---- Fuller P. Hale died Feb. 5,1901 ----.
Babe of E. D. & Deborah Hale died April 13, 1899.
E.D. Hale of Boones Creek, Tenn. and Deborah Masengill of Bluff City, Tenn.
married on Dec. 23, 1897 at her home by Rev. P. P. Kinser.

There is an Old graveyard at Gray's Station in the garden at Jim Grays that has
Hale graves in it. ( I have not copies of these stones). (E.R.W.).

The first Baptist Church organized in Washington County was supposed to have bee
the Cherokee Creek Church before 1783. However the oldest records found of the
Sinking Creek Baptist Church. Among the Cherokee Creek Church records Nicholas
Hale was one of the first members. ( Goodspeed'd History of Washington Co. ( East
Tenn.) page 891). ( note by E.R.W).

Shipley Graveyard in Washington Co. ---- R. L. Hale born Aug. 22- 1869 died
Feb. 27-1908.

Richard Murrell married Sarah Hale of Washington County Tennessee. ( Goodspeed'c

History of Marshall County Tennessee page 1220).

North Carolina Grants 1783-1793. Vol. 1.- Inc. in Vol. 15. page 104. Moses
Hail--- 117 acres. Washington County. .

Plat and Survey book of Washington County. -----No. 130 John Hale, Occupant
Claim. By virtue of an occupant claim I have surveyed for John Hale 230 acres
of land in Hawkins County on the Main road leading from Dodson foard to Mossey
Creek joining Micajah Lee tract of land. Beginning on a post 0ak on said Lees
line running south 152 poles to Thomas Lees corner Post oak then with his said
west 108 poles to pine then a long the same south 65 poles to post oak then south
20 poles to postoak then west 80 poles to post oak then No. 150 poles to Black
Oak then Straight to the Beginning. Surveyed 26th August 1808.   Jeremiah Killingdworth, Lazarus Gulley ---- C. B.Scale 100 poles to the inch.   --- Wm. Paine,
D.S. 6th Dist. filed in the office 31 Aug. & Recorded 29th Sept. 1808.

Same reference as above. No. 137. Frederock Hale Occupant Claim. ---Surveyed
this 2nd day of April 1808 a tract of land for Frederick Hale situate in the sixth
District in Greene County. Beginning at a hickory etc. etc. Adj. William Gibsons
line. Survey made pursuant to 36th Section of Act of Assembly issued 3rd Dec.
1807. Moses Raves and William Hale. ---- C. B. Scale 100 acres to the inch.

Same reference as above --- No. 456. Ruth Hale, Survey No. 389. in Sixth Dist.
dated Jan. 8- 1810 founded on warrant No. 551. 30th Oct.1778. Surveyed for Ruth
Hale assigneec of John Kennedy who was assignee of Elisha Embree who was assignee
of George Swingle assignee of John Swingle 320 acres of land, assignee of
Nathaniel Taylor who was assignee of James Stewart. In Sixth Dist. of Washington
County on Boones Creek. adjoining George Russell on Thos. Hawks line, also to
heirs of George Nolen line and on John Bacons line. To an old survey granted to
Joseph Duncan. Jesse Bacon. and Mark Hale, C.C.

Same reference No. 553. Pursuant to Duplicate of a land warrant issued to John
Carter entry taker for the County of Sullivan in the State of North Carolina
to William Ingram for 500 acres 1779, entered the 8th day of Jany 1779. Surveyed
for George Hale ( Hail) Assignee of Thomas Ingram heirs assignee of William
Ingram, dec'd, a tract of land in 6th Dist. of Hawkins County in Carters Valley
above the town of Rogersville and on both sides of the two roads commonly called
Sevier road and Carters Valley road, adjoining William Crocketts old improvemnets
including David Crocketts Junr and William Kinhard Inprovements joining the
lands of George Geevers Richard Mitchell ( formerly Thomas Amoss) John Mitchell
and Richard Mitchell. etc. etc. John Stearns and Marrok Hilton.

Same reference as above.-----No. 646 Henderson Clark. Sixth District. No. 552.
dated Nov. 1810. land on Nolochucky River in Washington County. Isaac Henley
and William Clark. C. C.

Mr. Jim Fulwider of Fall Branch in Washington County, Tenn. says that Elizabeth
L. Whitlock the second wife of Lewis Hale, and that she was Elizabeth L. McCrary
sister of his grandfather. (E.R.W.)

Joseph Hale married Ibby McAddams Dec. 24, 1815 in Washington County, Tenn.
John Hail married Ruth Hail Jan. 1- 1815 in Washington County. Tenn.
James Hail married Jane Gray in Washington County, Tenn. May 11- 1816.
Walter Hale married Nancy Smith Nov. 16, 1816 Washington County Tenn.
Henry Hail married Harriet Kincholow June 26, 1817 Washington County, Tenn.
Enoch Hale married Phoebe Hawes April 15, 1820 in Washington County, Tenn.

19

. Tombstone records from the Old Hale Graveyard in edge of Washington and Green Counties about one mile from Hawes Cross Roads. This is the Old Joseph or Landon Carter Hale graveyard. Sometime called Chase graveyard. Farm owned by Mrs. Cox.
Shadrack Chase, born May 27,1811 died Nov. 12- 1887.
Margaret wife of Shadrack Chase born Aug. 24, 1812 died Dec. 5-1853.
Delsenah consort of James E. Hale and daughter of Shad Chase born 1844 died 1864.
Samuel Hale born 1846 died July 14- 1858.
Thomas Hale born 1848 died July 10- 1858.
Mollie M. Hale born Feb. 4, 1838 died Feb. 18, 1884.
Infant Sallie E. Hale.
Shadrack G. Hale born Feb. 12- 1840 died Sept. 9,.1921.
L. C. Hale ( Landon Carter Hale) born Jan. 1- 1812 died April 19, 1878.
Hannah Ellis Hale born Aug. 8, 1813 died Oct. 23, 1890.
William C. Hale born Feb. 14, 1844 died May 23, 1918.
Emma Kiser Hale born 1848 died 1923.

PENSION RECORD OF AMON HALE --- Washington County Tennessee. File W.227.
Pensioner of 1840. The record of Amon Hale or Haile, the family used both spellings is furnished herein as found in the papers on file in pension claim, W-227 based upon his service in the Revolutionary War. Amon Hale was born June 16, 1759 in North Carolina and moved with his parents, when an infant to Baltimore County Maryland; the names of his parents are not shown. While a resident of Baltimore County Maryland he enlisted in August, served as a private in Captain Joshua Stephenson's Maryland Company, and continued for one year, engaged in guarding the magazine at Baltimore. No specific dates of this service were stated. He was allowed pension on his application executed April 17, 1833, at which time he resided in Washington County, Tennessee.
The soldier died December 4, 1843. Amon Hale married September 30-1785 Mary, whose maiden name is not shown. Soldier's widow, Mary applied for pension Dec. 8, 1843 at which time she was aged seventy-nine years; the date and place of her birth are not shown. Mary Hale was then a resident of Washington County, Tennessee The claim was allowed. After the death of her husband, Mary Hale lived in the house of her son, Robert G. Hale, She died there January 29, 1849 in Jonesboro, Tennessee. The names of the children of Amon Hale and his wife Mary, are shown as follows:

| | |
|---|---|
| Elizabeth Born Sept. 1-1786. | Mary born Dec. 14,1797. |
| Uratha born Sept. 11-1788. | Joshua born Feb. 10,1800. |
| Jesse W. born Oct. 16,1791. | Prisse born Aug. 8,1802. |
| Micajah B. born March 20,1793. | Amon C. born March 11,1805. |
| Robert G. born Nov. 16,1795. | Ruth born Nov. 11, 1807. |

The soldier was survived by eight children, their names not designated. The son Robert G. Hale, resided in Jonesboro, Tenn. in 1849; he stated then that the soldier's children were "scattered all over the western country"; he referred to a granddaughter who was with the widow, Mary, when she came to his house to live, but he did not give her name; reference was made also, to a son-in-law, whose wife was deceased, but his name was not stated. ---- signed A.D. Hiller. Assistant to Administrator. ( Veterans Administration. Washington D. C. Sept. 29-1934.).

Will of Nicholas Hale as on file in Washington County Tenn. Will Book 1.page118.
He is styled Nicholas Hale Senr. --- In the name of God Amen, I Nicholas Hale Senr, of Washington County and State of Tennessee being of a sound mind and memory thanks be to Almighty God do by these presents make and ordain this my last will, and testament in manner following (viz): First -- I have given to my Six sons Richard, William, Nicholas, Nathan, Amon, and Joshua heretofore their full portion in lieu and other property and so my will is my six sons above mentioned to receive one dollar out of my estate each of them and no more. Secondly, after all my lawfull debts being paid my will is my three daughters Elizabeth Cage Ruth Hale and Sarah Gray to have the remainder of my personal

ostate to be equally divided  among them.
Thirdly -- A certain tract or parcel of land lying  Thomas Murrays line and Thomas
Barrons line and  Michael Eddlemons line supposed to be between  eighty or ninety
acres to be equally divided between  the heirs of John Hale Dec'd, and reason
for this is the  said John Hale dec'd estate being a piece of land  I gave to
my son Amon Hale and he sold it to the said John Hale and they have never had any
title from me for it yet so my will is to leave it as above.
Fourthly - - my will is that my Mallajo man  Bob at my death be set at his liberty
and become a  free man --- except there be a crop on hand and  then at the comming
in of the crop to be set at his liberty.
Fifthly --- my will is that my son Richard Hale  have the whole managing of my
affairs wherefrom I set my hand and seal this 29th day  of April 1807.
Test                         his                          Nicholas Hale , Senr. (SEAL)
Loyd # Ford ,  George  X Jackson , Rolina Berry(?).
   his mark                 mark
   The foregoing will was proven in open court by the Oaths of Loyd Foard, and
George Jackson two of the subscribing witnesses thereto  at July session 1818 and
ordered to be recorded.

The pension record of Nathan Hale in short is as follows ---- Nathan Hale applied
for Pension in Giles County, Tenn. Nov. 1832. He was born in North Carolina
1757 when a child moved with his father to Baltimore Maryland. He enlisted while
in Baltimore County in Co. Joshua Stephenson's Maryland Regiment. Richard Hale
of Giles County also deposes that he was in Revolutionary War. Nathan Hale says
his father moved after the Revolution to Tennessee. They lived first in Washington
County and then Nathan moved to Giles County.

 Nicholas Hale Pension report. Applied for  Pension for Revolutionary service
while living in Davidson County, Oct. 27-1832. Then nearly 70 years old, there-
fore born about 1762. He enlisted and served while living in Washington County N.
C. now Tennessee in 1780 under Capt. Sevier. Col. Robertson's Regiment. Moved
after the Revolution to Davidson County Tennessee.

Among the Survey and Play Books for 6th Dist. of Tennessee. in the State Land
Office at Nashville, Tenn.  Page 445. Survey No. 2267. By virtue of an entry made
in the surveyors office of the sixth district of No. 921 dated the 24th of December 1811 founded on a warrant of No. 1420 dated 2nd July 1810. Surveyed for
Joseph Hale assignee of Nathan Shipley assignee of James Miller one hundred acres
of land in Sixth District of Washington County  on waters of Kindricks Creek on a
ridge William Barrons  corner, adjoingin William Jackson and Charles Bacons line.
Also Charles Durhams line. Jany 15, 1812.

Page 449. No. 2276. By virtue of entry made in the surveyors office of 6th Dist.
No. 3628 dated 15th day of Dec. 1816 founded on a  certificate No. 134 dated
25th day of July 1815 issued by the commissioner of East Tennessee to George
Ridley I have surveyed for Abdenigo Hale assignee of George Vincent assingee of
George Ridley 120 acres of land in 6th Dist. Washington County head waters of
Lick Creek adjoining said Hales line etc. etc. Leroy Hale, and Hezekiah Hale
C. C. surveyed Feb. 14-.1817.

The Old Shadrack and Meshack  Hale graveyard is located on the farm of Mr. Charles
Cox only about one and half miles from Fall Branch in Washington County. The
graveyard is just over the line in Greene County but the land appears to have the
county line to cut it into.  There are no stones with markings in this plot. They
are just rocks and no inscriptions. The Cox family purchased it  from Enoch
Hale son of Meshack Hale about sixty-nine years ago. ( note the will of
Meshack Hale this note book for mention of this graveyard).

Washington County Tennessee Census report 1830 on a few of tho Hales. ( from Census reports Washington D. C. ). ----- John Hale of Thomas, had one male between the ages of 20 and 30 years ( includes head of family) and two females under five years of age and one female between ages of twenty and thirty ( includes head of family).

Thomas Hale Sr. had one male between ages of 15 and 20. one between ages of 50 and 60 years. One female between 20 and 30 and one female between 50 and 60 years. Ned Hale's family. ( does not show how many).

. George Hale had two males between 10 and 15 years, one between 20 and 30 years and one between 60 and 70 years. also one female between 15 and 20 years and one between 50 and 60 years.

Mark Hale had two males between 5 and 10 years, one between 10 and 15 years, one between 15 and 20 years, one between 20 and 30 years, one between 40 and 50 years; also two females under five years, two between 15 and 20 years and one between 30 and 40 years.

Joseph Hale had one male between 60 and 70 years; also one female between 10 and 15 years, one between 15 and 20 years, two between 20 and 30 years and one between 50 and 60 years.

Henry Hale had two males under 5 years, one between 5 and 10 years, one between 10 and 15 years and one between 30 and 40 years. Also two females between 5 and 10 years and one between 30 and 40 years.

Chenowth Hale had one male between 20 and 30 years and one female between 20 and 30 years.

Zochariah Hale had. two males between 5 and 10 years, one between 10 and 15 years and one between 40 and 50 years of age. also one female between 10 and 15 years, one between 15 and 20 years and one between 30 and 40 years.

Enoch Hale is shown in the report.

Jack Hale, Amon Hale, Charles Hale, Joshua Hale, Amon Hale Sr, Archibald Hale, Chase Hale, Leroy Hale, George Hale, Mary Hale, James Hale, Robert G. Hale. and Walter Hale. Many of these had families, a few did not.

Washington County Census report I have made note from the 1840 of those in addition to the above. I have only included notes of interest and appearing new information . Henry Hale, Alison Hail, Edmond Hail, James Hail of Bumpass, William Hail, Amon Hale aged 83 at this time. Lilburn Hail was in 5th Regiment of the county taken by G. W. Millet ahd is shown as having two males under 5 years, one between 10 and 15 years, and one between 15 and 20 years. also one female between 15 and 20 years, and one between 20 and 30 years.

Among the North Carolina Grants and deeds from Individuals in the Watauga Purcha 1775-1782 page 64 Tenn. State Land Office. Nov. 24- 1775 Charles Roberson to Robert Young lands witnessed by Haile Talbot.

Mrs. John E. Hale was the daughter of William Gannaway Brownlow at one time Governor of Tennessee. ( M.S.S. records on Gannaway family of "Virginia by Katherine K. Adams).

Minute Book Washington County Tenn. 1788 May. page 322. Mesack Hale on Jury. Page 392 -- 1789 Aug. A deed from Shadrack Hale and Mary Hale for 140 acres to William McPike was acknowledged in open court Let it be registered.  On page 329, One other deed from Shadrack and Mary Hale to Joe Poteet for 200 acres of land was acknowledged in open court and ordered recorded.

The Lewis Hale place in the edge of Sullivan and Washington Counties is now known as the Galloway place. Hale sold it to Willards and they in turn sold it to the Galloways.

Among the census reports in Washington D. C. for the year 1850 I make note
Aug. 14--- Messick Hale aged 19 years a student born in Tennessee.
Mark Hale aged 61 years born in Tenn.    Polly Hale.  Cheneth Hale aged 43 years
and Nancy Hale aged 43 years both born in Tenn. Merah Hale aged 43 years born in
Kentucky. Elizabeth Hale age 80 years born in Maryland living with Henry Hale and
Mary his wife.  Mary Hale aged 97 years born in Maryland. ( this is Mary wife
of Meshack Hale).

Among the Legislative Papers on file in the State Archives Nashville, for Washing-
ton County there is one dated 1829 regarding the county line of Green and
Washington, on the one from Washington County I find Enoch Hale, Meshack Hale
Senr., Mashack Hale Jr., Shadrack Hale, Amon Hale.  On the one from Greene County
I find Mashack Hale Senr.

One Mary Hale married William Henry Henderson. (Who was she or who was her
parents?)

Lewis Hale buried at Fall Branch, Tennessee, Washington County, in what is known
as the Hopper Graveyard or the Old Baptist Church Cemetery only a few yards
off the main highway right in the little settlement of Fall Branch. The ·Hale stones
at this place read: Elizabeth consort of Lewis Hail born April 8- 1798 died Nov.
15, 1863;  Lewis Hale born July 5, 1794 died Sept. 18, 1880 aged 86 years 2 mo,
and 13 days;  Elizabeth Hail born Mar. 15, 1802 died Nov. 12, 1888; Sarah daughter of Lewis and Elizabeth Hale born June 16, 1867 died Feb. 3- 18__; Annaliza
daughter of Lewis and Elizabeth Hale born April 24, 1839 died Dec. 15, 1856.

Washington County Tennessee. Land Office Nashville, Grants --- No.13651 George
Hale; 25751 George Hale; 25863 Lewis Hale; 27473 Geo. Hale;  27878 James C. Hale
heirs; 29874 Chase Hale.

Washington County  Grants, Land Office, Nashville --- 1817--Abednego Hale; 1849
Enoch Hale; 1827 George Hale; 1849 George S. Hale;1867 Hiram D. Hale; 1819 James
Hale; 1851 Jas. C. Hale heirs; 1885 James E. Hale; 1817 Joseph Hale; 1817 Joseph
Hale; 1847 Lewis Hale. ( number represents year of grant).

Sept. 24-1832 received of Meshack Hail for collection one note of ____ on Joshua
Boran for the amount of seven dollars and seventy-five cents this day and ¡date
above mentioned. ( papers of George B. Hale of Johnson City, Tenn).

Recd. of J. L. Whitlock the amount in full of the Estate Belonging to Joseph
Marshall deceased this 25 day of November 1853. Frances H. Marshall. ( Geo.B.
Hale's papers).

Recd. of Elizabeth Bragg for 1836, 8, 76 this tax on district No. 15, A. James
Shipp. ( Papers of G. B. Hale).

Received of Lewis Hale administrator of David Bragg, deceast one dollar and
twenty-five cents in full of my part and James Tickens which  I am guardian for
this 18th June 1851. John Tickens. ( G. B. Hale papers).

Received of Mary Hail, Executors of the estate of Meshack Hail deceased the full
amount of my part of seven negroes left by Meshack Hail decd. according to his
will to be equally divided between a part of his heirs namely--- Lewis, Nancy,
Charles, Enoch, Sary, Meshack, Mary, Jackson ( commas inserted), Washington
one negro boy received by me James Haws and Nancy Haws April the 29th 1834---
Joseph Howard. ( Geo B. Hales papers).
23

This day I have bargained and sold unto Lewis Hale all the right title claim
and interest that I have in a certain roan mare taken from me in the time of
the war being between ten and fifteen years of ago as I do not know her age
exactly but the mare can be proved by a number of persons by a scar in her eye-
lid when sold my claim to Lewis Hale for Hassie Rassiour, witness my hand and
seal this the seventh day of September 1868 Elisa A. Howar. ---- James C. Ranger.
( Papers of Geo. B. Hale).

A letter June 5, 1863 written from Bell Buckle to Mrs. Elizabeth Whitlock by
J. V. Hulse. ( Geo. B. Hale papers).
A letter dated April 15, 1863 Vicksburg, Miss to his wife by J. S. Whitlock also
one dated Feb. 25, 1863 from same ;   ( Geo B. Hale Papers).

Among the records of the Sinking Creek .Baptist Church, Washington County,
are found. Sept.10-1785 Meshack Hail was Deakon, Timothy Tracy, elder. Also
letters of dismissal to Agnes Talbot wife of Mathew Talbot Senr. ( Agnes was the
last wife of Mathew Talbot. ---- E.R.W).    June 29- 1834 Sister Temperance Hale
from Pig River, Franklin County Virginia-- recommended to Sinking Creek.  Among the
register of members 1787 Meshack Hail and his wife Catherine.

Richard Hale married Mary Cox, of Sullivan County. He was son of John Hale, a
pioneer of Washington County and a Revolutionary Soldier.  Richard and Mary
his wife had six children one of which was James Born 1813 married Mary Ann Moore
1841 and had 9 children.    Richard Hale was 1812 private in Capt. James Landers
Company 4th (Bayless) Reg. of East Tenn. Drafted Militia Service began Nov. 13-
1814 and ended May 18- 1815. ( From Mary McCowan's records of 1812 records).

SOME TAX LIST NOTES,WASHINGTON COUNTY---
1795- Capt. Melvanes Co. -- Abednego Haile,  237 acres Washington Co. Boones
Creek o pole free and 4 slaves.
  1798 Capt. Shipleys Co.-- Meshack Hail son of Shadrack Hail  1 white poll 100 acres.
    "    "     "         "-- Nicholas Hail Senr. 1 black poll 272 acres.
    "    "     "         "-- George Hail Jun. 1 white poll 200 acres.
    "    "     "      .  "-- Henry Hail son of John. 1 white poll 100 acres.
    "    "     "         "-- John Hail  no polls 84 acres.
    "    "     "         "-- Joseph Hail, elder, 20 polls  836 acres.
    "    "     "         "-- Amon Hail  1 white poll no land.
  1795 Capt. Murey's Co.  Joseph Hale son of George 100 acres West Sinking Cr.  1
white poll.
  1795 Capt. Murey's Co.  John Haile 92 acres on West Sinking Cr. no white polls.
    "     "      "      "  William Haile 200 acres West Sinking Creek. 1 white poll.
    "     "      "      "  Nathan Haile 200 acres on West Sinking Creek. 1 white poll.
    "     "      "      "  Nicholas Haile Sr. 272 acres ( 3 tracts) West Sinking
Creek. 1 black poll.
  1795 Capt. Murey's Co.  Meshack Haile 420 acres East Sinking Creek.
    "  :   "      "      "  Jemina Haile, no land 2 negroes.
    "     "      "      "  Administratrix of Nicholas Haile Estate 200 acres on
West Sinking Creek 500 acres on Kendricks Creek.
  1795 Capt. Murey's Co. Shadrack Haile 100 acres  Head of Clear Cork of Lick Creek
and 1 poll.
  1795 Capt. Murey's Co.  Samuel Haile 100 acres West Sinking Creek 100 acres on
East Sinking Creek. 1 white poll.
  1795 Capt. Murey's Co. George Haile Junr. on Cedar Creek 226 acres.
    "     "      "      "  Josephiner Haile ( elder) 836 acres Cedar Creek. 1 white
poll.
  1795 Capt. Murey's Co. George Haile Senr. 150 acres on East fork Cedar Creek 50
acres no polls.

1795, Capt. Murey's Company, Richard Haile, 110 acres West Sinking Creek also 120 acres in Sullivan County. 1 poll.

1795 Capt. Murey's Company, Joshua Haile. nothing said about him.
"     "      "        "     , Little Meshack Haile 100 acres in Greene County on Lick Creek.

1795 Capt. Murey's Company, Abednego Haile, 300 acres and 45 acres ( 2 tracts) Lick Creek.   He was too old for poll. and called Abednego the older.

1796 Capt. Melvin's Company. Washington County. Abednego Haile, 1 white poll 5 Blacks 232 acres land 1 horse stud.

1795 Capt. Shipley's Company. George Haile Junr. 1 white poll 2 black and 220 acres
"     "        "         "     , Nathan Haile, 1 white poll 200 acres.
"     "        "         "     , Meshack Haile 1 white poll 420 acres.
"     "        "         "     , George Haile Senr. 1 black poll 200 acres.
"     "        "         "     , Samuel Hail  1 hict poll 175 acres.

1797 Capt. Biddles Company, Abednego Haile  1 white poll 100 acres.

1797 Capt. Calvert's Company, Jesse Haile, nothing shown.

E. B. Hale M. D. born Washington County, Tenn. 12/14/1838 son of James C. and Elmira (Beacon) Hale. Had six children. ( History of Hamblen Co. by Goodspeed page 1204-5).

Will of John Kincheloe of Washington County  Book 1. page 426 mentions "To John Hale is he live with his grandmother untill 21. etc. " "To Maneroee Hale cow andcalf if she live with her grandmother"

Henry Hale was 53 years of age in 1850 was a Farmer. He was born in North Caroline. His wife was Harriet Hale aged 53 years in 1850 born in North Carolina. Living in their house in 1850 was Joseph L. Hale aged 21 years, Henry Hale aged 16 years, Martha Hale, aged 14 years, Sarah Hale aged 12 years, Harriet Hale aged 11 years. All born in North Carolina. ( Census of Washington Co. Tenn. 1850).

George T. Hale aged 50 years born in Tenn. living in Washington Co. Tenn. 1850. His wife was Temperance Hale aged 45 years born in Tenn. and living in their house was Andrew J. Hale aged 19 years, George W. Hale, aged 16 years, John A. C. Hale aged 14 years, W. C. Hale aged 10 years, Mary R. Hale aged 7 years, and James F. Hale aged 6 years, all born in Tenn. ( U.S. Census 1850 Washington Co.)

In 1850 Henry Hale aged 36 years born in Tenn. Mary Hale aged 35 years born in Tenn and living in their house was -- Harriet Hale aged 10 years, John Hale aged 9 years, Eliza Hale aged 9 years, Chinowth Hale aged 6 years, Daniel Hale aged 5 years, Thomas aged 1 year, Elizabeth Hale aged 80 years and Frances Chenoth aged 60 years. The last two born in Maryland and the rest in Tennessee. ( U.S. Census 1850).

John Hale applied for Pension while living in Bledsoe County Tenn. He was a Revolutionary Soldier. Applied while living in Bledsoe County Tenn 1833. He was born in Bedford County Virginia 1753 or 1754. Enlisted in Bedford County Va. 1776 Volunteered in Capt. Harry Buford's Co. Lieut. John Fields, Ensign Abram Sharp. He had 24 months service. His discharge burned in Blount County 1803. After the war he moved to Wythe County Virginia then to Greene County Tenn then to Washington County Tennessee and from there to Blount Co. Tenn. and then to Bledsoe County Tenn. in 1813. ( Pension Reports in Veterans Administration Bureau Washington. D. C.

There is a little settlement called $^H$ales located in 15th District of Washington County ( 1934) almost directly north of Jonesboro about five or six miles from Jonesboro. (E.R.W).

Mrs. Mollie Odel and Mrs. J. H. Hale of Haws Cross Roads in Washington County have given the following notes: Place wher Mrs. Orvil Cox lives is originally the Hale farm. ----- Landon Carter Hale was grandfather of Mrs. Odel. Landon Carter Hale had James Ellis Hale who married first Delach Chase and second a Miss Ferguson; Harrison Hale married Mary Wallace; Shadrack Hale never married, went to Texas and lived many years, returned to Tenn and died; Hutts Hale married Julia Register and went to Texas; William Hale married Emy Kiser; Two small children died in infancy named Sam and Tom; Matilda Elizabeth Hale married a Mr. Bolton; Sarah Hale married a Mr. King ( is mother of Mrs Pate); Mary Hale (Called Polly) never married. ----- Landon Carter Hale married Hannah Ellis ( this is the father of this set of children). (E.R.W).

Among the records of the Fall Branch Baptist Church at Fall Branch I have found -----On Saturday July 28, 1827 the members dismissed from the Double Spring Baptist Church and organized--- . Amon Hail was ordained Deacon on the same day. April 1829 Jeremiah Hale permitted to exercise a public gift and David D. Shackleford have license to preach. Sept. 12 James Poindexter made pastor. Nov. 27 Jeremiah Hail ordained to the Ministry. June 12- 1869 After sermon by Rev. Jeese Hale Mrs. Hannah Hale was received by letter from Limestone Church. Laura Hale was baptized Mar. 13- 1870. Feb. 13-1869 Dr. P. P. Hale deacon dismissed by letter and Caroline S Hale deaconess dismissed by letter. James E. Hale 1869 dismissed by letter. Landon Carter Hale excluded for treating the church with combompt and drinking Feb. 1872. Elizabeth Hale, Lydia A. Hubbard, Mary Hale and $^H$annah Hale by letter June 12-1869. Jeremiah Halo sent to Cherokee Church Jan. 7- 1832. Feb. 1843 David Hale permitted to exercise a public gift. Dec. 12- 1846 $^D$avid B. Hale ordained to the Ministry. Among the members by name Hale on the list I found---- Meshack Hale, Lewis Hale, James $^H$ale, Enoch Hale, Mary Hale, Eliza Hale, Nancy Hale, Henry Hale, Sarah Hale, Anna Hale, Isbella G. Hale, Eliza M. Hale.

DEEDS IN WASHINGTON COUNTY TENNESSEE IN THE NAME OF HALE:

| Book | Page | Name | Acres | Year. |
|------|------|------|-------|-------|
| 17 | 130 | Henry Halo to John Halo __a | | 1821 |
| 17 | 130 | Henry Hale to Thomas Hle | | 1821 |
| 17 | 131 | Henry Hale to Solomon Hale | | 1821 |
| 17 | 132 | Henry Hale to Joseph Chinoth | | 1821 |
| 13 | 441 | Archibald Hale from Ruth Hale | | 1814 |
| 14 | 23 | M rk Hale from Ruth $^H$alo | | 1814 |
| 14 | 67 | Abednigo Halo from Uriah Hunt | | 1814 |
| 14 | 102 | Henry,John, & Joseph send of $^R$uth from Ruth Halo | | 1814 |
| 15 | 258 | Abednego Hale to Stephen Hale | | 1817 |
| 15 | 262 | Abednego Halo to Guy Hale | | 1817 |
| 15 | 260 | Abednego Hale to Burd Hale | | 1817 |
| 12 | 363 | Ruth $^H$alo from State of $^T$onn. | | 1811 |
| 16 | 28 | Guy Halo, Stephen Hale to Thos Bandland | | 1818 |
| 17 | 128 | Henry Hale to Stephen Hale | | 1821 |
| 17 | 129 | Henry Hale to Henry Chinoth | | 1821. |
| 5 | 118 | Richard $^H$alo from Nicholas Hale (father of Richd) | | 1792 |
| 5 | 139 | William Halo from Nicholas Hale his father | | 1792 |
| 7 | 289 | George Halo to Alexander Hail | | 1795 |
| 7 | 335 | Meshack Hailo to Henry Bogant | | 1795 |
| 7 | 354 | Meshack Hale to John Hale | | 1795 |
| 6 | 561 | Nicholas $^H$ailo to Elizabeth Stephenson | | 1800 |

26

| Book | Page | Name | Acres | Year |
|------|------|------|-------|------|
| 6 | 563 | Nathan Hale to Elizabeth Stephenson | | 1800 |
| 6 | 601 | Amon Hale to Wm. Slaughter | | 1800 |
| 7 | 54 | Abddnego Hale to Phillip G. Pearce | | 1794 |
| 5 | 39 | Samuel Hale from William Dotson | | 1792 |
| 5 | 44 | Abednego Hale from North Carolina Grant | | 1790 |
| 5 | 65 | Nicholas Hale grant from N. C. ( Nicholas Jr) | | 1791 |
| 5 | 116 | Nathan Hale from Nicholas his father | | 1792 |
| 13 | 84 | Meshack Hale to Zachariah Hale | | 1812 |
| 13 | 227 | Nathan Hale to Alexander Hale | | 1812. |
| 13 | 441 | Ruth Hale to Archibald Hale | | 1814. |
| 14 | 23 | Ruth Hale to Mark Hale | | 1814 |
| 9 | 269 | Shadrack Hale Jr. from Shadrack Sr.his father | | 1803. |
| 8 | 228 | Joseph Haile to Isaac Bacon | | 1805 |
| 8 | 311 | Nicholas Hale Sr. to Nathan Haile his son | | 1801 |
| 9 | 197 | Samuel Hale to Joseph Hale | | 1799 |
| 7 | 16 | Alexander Hale from N.C. a Grant | | 1794 |
| 7 | 289 | Alexander Hail from Geo Hail | | 1795 |
| 7 | 354 | John Hale from Meshack Hale | | 1795 |
| 20 | 151 | John C. Hale and wife to Jno. Cox | | 1834 |
| 20 | 328 | Byrd B. Hale to Isaac Horton | | 1835 |
| 20 | 371 | John Hale to Nancy Hale ( others) ( Colored) | | 1835 |
| 19 | 36 | Mark Hale to Jeremiah Hale | | 1830 |
| 22 | 232 | Shadrack Hale to Landon Carter Hale | | 1838 |
| 23 | 36 | Charles Hale to James Haws | | 1839 |
| 23 | 57 | Elizabeth Hale to Abraham Jones | | 1839 |
| 17 | 299 | Amon Hale to Chase Hale | | 1823 |
| 17 | 429 | Leroy Hale to John Copass | | 1825 |
| 17 | 498 | Henry Hale & Jno. C. Hale to Jno. C. & Jos. Hale | | 1826 |
| 18 | 340 | Arch Hale to James Moore    Agreement | | 1829 |
| 19 | 19 | Thos Hale to Clauda Hale | | 1830 |
| 19 | 122 | Aaron Hale to Aiken Fitzgerald | | 1831 |
| 19 | 350 | Geo. Hale to Wm. Hale | | 1833 |
| 17 | 503 | Arch Hale from Henry & Jno. Hale et al. | | 1826 |
| 35 | 290 | Finley Hale from Wm. K. Hale | | 1855 |

NOTE: There are some hundred or more deeds in Washington County in the name Hale. The above are selected as those of most important one -- E.R.W.

Marriages in Washington County ----- Meshack Hail and Jane Kennedy Oct. 27- 1831.
Joseph Hale and Sarah Broyles  Aug. 9- 1833
Wm. Hale and Elizabeth Biddle March k0-1836
Allison Hale and Elizabeth Kinchaloe Nov. 26- 1836
Elizabeth Hale and Therwood Vaughn Oct.20-1835.
Sarah Hale and James Billingsley May 24-1825
F. Hail to M. Bacon May 25-1839.
J. Hale and E. Barkley May 16- 1839.
Wm. Hail and S. Buckingham Oct.20-1840.
J. C. Hail & E. Brown  March 3- 1842.
A. C. L. Hail and C. Sherfey Feb. 13- 1842.
R. Hail and E. Spurgin  Oct. 13- 1843.
H. Hail and E. Sherfey  July 20- 1843.
A. Hale and R. Good  March 16-1844.

Washington County, Tenn. Deeds. 1825. Division of estate of Meshack Hale.
to John Hair and wife deed. April 15-1825. Book 17 page 444. Zachariah Hale,
Margaret Hinkle, Isham Matlock, Nancy Matlock, Ransom Matlock, Barbara Matlock,
Thomas Grosham, Elizabeth Grosham, heirs of Meshac Hale deceased. John Hair
and wife Asa (Ara) --- She a dau. of Meshack Hale.

George Hale's will. Wife Elanor. divided among children at her death--- children
not named. June 8- 1835.

Jackson Hale's will--- wife Elizabeth. son Elijah Hale, Daughter Harriet Hale.
April 30- 1839 witnessed by Allison Heale.

Will of Elizabeth Hale, dated Oct. 11- 1820 proved July 1827 --- To Elizabeth,
Richard Chenoth and Hale Chenowth each Household Goods. Elizabeth wife of
Thomas Hale and to Henry Hale son of Thomas . . To Lucy Chenoth wife of
Nicholas Chenoth a set of china. Mentions men of color Richard, Samuel, Elizabeth
dau. of Lucy, Botsy and her dau. Botsy. called Hale.

Will of Joseph Hale.-- July 17- 1843 proved 1844.-- son Benjamine, daughter Lucy,
Daughter Susannah Cade, daughter Louisa (?), wife Isabella, son Landon C. Hale.
Dau. Martha Jackson, Dau Nancy Guess, Dau. Mary Billingsly, Dau. Ann Hale,
Dau. Sarah Billingsly. Gives Martha land she lives on in Perry County, Tenn.
Sons Benjamine and Landon Hale Executors,

John Hale's Will. July 21- 1846. Wife Elizabeth , plantation and if she marru
again to be divided among hiers of John Hale. Witnessed by Thomas Hale.

Canday Hale's will. dated June 21- 1848 proved July Term 1849. son Richard,
dau. Elizabeth. Rest of bodily Heirs D. Maliday, Sarah, Hannah Jordan, Eleart,
Jane and two heirs of my daughter Dorcus to wit Samuel Franlin and Dorcus and
Hubbard. Appnts Jordan Elbert Hale a son Executor. Witnessed by Hirman D. Hale
and Benj. Shipley. ·

Will of Hannah Hale. Dec. 28- 1872. son F. D. Hale and son Wm. K. Hale.

Chase Hale' will. dated April 27- 1872 proved 1876. wife Clary Hale,
Margaret Jackson and heirs. Her husband John W. Jackson, Wlizabeth Hale wife of
my son William Hale, Polly Ann Jackson, Hannah Cox, Ruth Mitchell, Son Geo. Hale
deceased. Jas W. Cox son of Sally Cox decd. daughter Susan Hale exec.

Henry Hale's Will. Wife Jane Hale, son Thomas S. Hale, son Samuel Hale, dau.
Nancy Ruth Hale, a - - dau. Ellen Pherson, Dau. Mary Douglas, dau. Jeese
Biddle, dau. Jane Biddles, son William. Hale. granddau. Mary Jane Hale daughter
of Wm. Hale. dated Jany 15- 1870.

·
Chinowth Hale's will. son Harvey N. Hale;wife Nancy Hale, children Thos Hale,
Harriet Hale, Fannie Curtis, Louisa Sells, and Rena Hale dated April 22- 1877
proved Aug. 1877.

Henry Hale's Will. Wife Harriet. Family : Mattha Hale, Sarah Hale, and Harriet
Hale my granddaus. Smith H. Hale, Joseph L. Hale, and Finley Hale my 3
youngest sons. Son William K. Hale, eldest son Franklin D. Hale, son-in-law
Jackson Hale, daughter Mary Board. Oct. 1-1850 proved Nov. 1850.

Will of William Hale, Sept. 28, 1855 proved Nov. 1855. Heirs Hannah Ligon Hale,
John B. Hale, Mary Hale, Wm.C. Hale. Father Geo. Hales estate is mentioned.
Appointed Hiram D. Hale Exec. Witnessed by William C. Hale and Howell Jenkins.

Martha Hale's will. Proved Jany 1856. Mentions Franklin D. Hale, Joseph L.
Hale. "my father lands where Harriet Hale now lives", my brothers William K,
Smith H. and Finley D. Hale. Brother Joseph L. Hale and Wm. K. Hale Exec.

Archibald Hale's will. dated March 24, 1854 proved 1855 in Jany. --- Wife
Mary Hale, daughter Minervia Slaven, daughter Ruth Allison, daughter Martha Hunt,
daughter Emalene Hale, daughter Margaretta Bowman, daughter Mary Brown, daughter
Amanda Jane Pritchett, daughter Thelma Duncan, grandson John Hale son of Allison
Hale, son David Hale widow and Lucinda is her name. To David's son John. My sons
Abednego and William Hale exec.

Will of George Hale Senr. April 30- 1805, probated Aug. session 1805.--- Wife
Ann Hale. His children. grand-dau. Susannah Hale ( dau. of son Geo.), son Samuel
Hale, dau. Elizabeth, dau. Ann, son Geo. Other children not named. Witnessed
by Nicholas Hale Senr and Jesse Crouch.

Henry Hale's Will. Ocy. 11- 1820 proved Jany 1822.--- Sister Elizabeth Hale.
The following free persons of color the rest of estate Maria, Lydia, Thomas,
John, Stephen, Solomon, Canada and Lucy Hale who call themselves by the surname
of Hale, who were by me liberated. To Joseph Chennoth land, To Henry Chenowth
lands, To Nicholas Chenowth several tracts of land. Nicholas Chenowth and
James Gray, Exec.

Joseph Hale's will. 10th April 1817. proved 1822 Jany. --- Brother Henry
Hale, Sister Elizabeth Hale, Elizabeth Chenoth daughter of Nicholas Chenowth,
my nephew Nicholas Chenowth. signed Joseph Hale, Henry Hale and Elizabeth Hale,
witnessed by John Dett, George Greshan.

Some notes on marriages in Washington County.---- John W. Brown and Maragret
Kinchelow Jan. 7- 1817 signed by Joshua Hail. ------- Joseph Chenowth &
Lidya Bean July 21- 1818 signed by Joshua S.Hale. ------ John Lucas to Susannah
Hale Sept. 1- 1790 signed by John Tipton.

**************************

SOME NOTES ON HALE FAMILY FROM
GREENE COUNTY
TENNESSEE

Settlement begun 1778 --- Lewis Brayles among first settlers and settled on Horse
Creek. A Church house was erected on Lick Creek at a very early day. The first
Baptist church was on Lick Creek organized 1793 &or 1794 --- Phillip Hale among
the first members. ( Goodspeed's History of Greene County page 881, 883).

James W. Hale was an attorney in Greene County, died 1842 ( Goodspeed's History
of Greene County page 885.).

1822 Petition of Citizens of Greene County relative to one Allen Gillespie a
J. P. of Greene County signed by Hugh D. Hale. J. P. ( Legislative papers in
Tenn. State Archives, Nashville, Box. 29).

29

North Carolina Grants, Tennessee Land Office. Phillip Hale page 119 Book B. 640 acres Warrant No. 265 on Little Chucky River.

North Carolina Grants Book C. page 138 Tenn. State Land Office, Nashville. Frederick Hail. 200 acres Greene County on North side Chucky River. Warrant No. 1400.

Greene County records at Greenville, Tenn. An old Book marked "Bills of Sales" Book. 2. page 281. Elijah Hale for consideration of five hundred dollars paid by A. M.Hall, Thomas M. Brandon, Wn. S. White and James Haws have this day transferred all right and title and interest that Mashack Hale, James Hall and his own to certain negroes now in possession of Mary Hale or was left to her by will of Meshack Hale deceased all. Sept. 6-1856.

Green  County Marriages ---- John B. Hale to Eliza F. King, Sept. 27- 1856.
James C. Hale to Margaret Bartles Mar. 17-1857.
Bird B. Hale and Margaret Scruggs, Jan. 26, 1858
Allen D. Hale and Angeline S. Temple, May 10-1858
Alexander Hale and Minerva Jane Shelton July 17-1858
James E. Hale and Delsenath Chase Dec. 31- 1858
Enoch Hale and Mary Jane Timmons Nov. 24- 1859
Killas Hale and Catherine Lawson Sept. 20, 1861.

In the census of 1830 for Greene County I have found several Hale entries: John Hale with one male under five years, one between 5 and 10 years, one between 30 and 40 years. Females one under five years, two between 20 & 30 years.
Alexander Hale with two males between 15 and 20 years, one between 60 and 70 years. also females one between 10 and 15 years, one between 15 and 20 years, one between 20 and 30 years and one between 50 and 60 years.
Hugh D. Hale Esqr. had one male between 5 and 10 years, one between 10 and 15 years, two between 15 and 20 years and one between 40 and 50 years. also one female under five years, one between 5 and 10 years, also one between 10 & 15 years and one between 30 and 40 years.
Joseph Hale with a family is shown in this report, also Thomas L. Hale with a family and Jesse W. Hale with a family.
Meshack Hale had one male between 10 & 15 years, one between 15 and 20 years, one between 30 and 40 years, one between 70 and 80 years also females one between 15 and 20 years and one between 50 and 60 years.

Greene County. Monday April 1-1861. The order her. to made appointing Enoch Hale agent for Mary Hale an aged infirm person is hereby rescinded and ordered to be for nothing held. ( Record Book at Greenville. Tenn. Minutes  1861 page 329).

Page 208 same book. Monday May 7- 1860. It appearing to the satisfaction of the court from the representation of Enoch Hale and William S. White Esqr., that Mary Hale from age and inability is wholly incompetent to manage and transact her business and c. The court is pleased to order and direct that Enoch Hale be and he is hereby appointed her agent with full power to attend to and manage her business and to hire out her negroes and to collect their wages and apply the same to the support of the said Mary Hale and to do and perform all other acts and things that may be necessary to be done as her agent in the premise (?).

A book labeled Note Book of Registrations and c. Beginning 1842 Jan. 7. page 2 -- Feb. 7-1842 Enoch Hale for the benefit of Nathan Gray of Grainger County negroes or personal property a fee of $1.00.

30

In the same book on page 3, Feb. 15- 1842 Hugh D. Hale (grantor) Geo. Jackson (Grantee) Greene Co. 200 acres fee of ⁅$1.25.

Deed Book Greene County, Tenn. Book 20 page 679 -- James Hale.

Box 1813 Road Papers Greene County. April Session Court. 1813. Christian Hale served on Jury.

Greene County Tenn. Census 1850 shows Joseph Hale aged 60 years a Farmer. born in Tennessee. Rebecca aged 44 years, and with them were living Catherine Hale aged 20 years, Alexander Hale 18 years, George Hale born 10 years, Charles Hale age 8 years and Young Hale aged 6 years. all born in Tennessee. ( U.S. Census report).

Abednego Hale aged 28 years born in Tenn, Catherine Hale aged 29 years, had in their household Allison aged 7 years, Samuel aged 4 years and Archibald Hale aged 2 years all born in Tennessee. ( Cesnus 1850 Washington D. C. ).

John Hale aged 38 years a farmer. wife Elizabeth aged 30 years, and in their house Martha J. aged 10 years, James aged 8 years, Samuel aged 7 years, William aged 3 years, all born in Tennessee. Also Malinda Morrow aged 32 years and John Hale aged 19 years a student. ( U.S. Consus report 1850 Greene Co.).

Joshua Hale aged 59 years  with Mary Ann aged 49 years and Milton aged 25 years a student, Harriot aged 19 yoars, and Alfred aged 18 years all born in Tenn. ( U.S. Census report Green Co. Washington D.C.).

Catherine Hale aged 56 years with Menirva Hale aged 23 years, James Hale aged 21 years and James Bible aged 18 years all born in Tennessee. ( U.S. Cuns., report for Greene County).

Hugh D. Hale aged 61 years born in Virginia. with Sarah . Hale aged 58 years Franklin Hale aged 18 years, and Hugh Hale aged 15 years all born in Tenn. (U.S. Census Report. Washington D.C.).

Philip Hale will April 22- 1814 proved 1819. Wife Catherine Hale. Son George Hale land in Knox County, Tenn. Sons Hugh D. Hale, Joseph Hale, Philip S. Hale, Thomas L. Hale and Patrick H. Hale. Daughters Sarah Neilson, Elizabeth D. Keith, Catherine D. Hale.

For Love and affection  Joseph Hale to daughter Catherine D.  Bevely and her son James Hale Bevely a negro girl.  June 18- 1853 ( Bill of Sales Book # 2 page 138. Greene County).

Henderick Majors of Lafayette Missouri appoints Thomas L. Hale of Greene County Tenn. attorney to seel lands in Green County on Lick Creek. April 13- 1836. (Greene Count Tenn records).

George S. Hale born May 23- 1840 moved to Cocke County 1870 and later to Green Co. and then to Hamblen Co. married Nancy J. Jones of Cocke Co. Dec. 12- 1867. Second of 5 sons of Joseph and Rebecca C. ( Landrum) Hale of Green Co. Rebecca died 1873 aged 66 years. Joseph commanded Co. under Gen. Jackson in war 1812 and elected Justice which he declined.  Joseph was son of Philip and Catherine (Douglas) Hale of Fauquier County Virginia. Moved to Greene Co. 1785. Philip's father was a brother of Capt. Nathaniel Hale who commanded a Company in the Revolutionary Army under Washington. ( Goodspeed's History of East Tenn. )

31

North Carolina Grants. Land Office , Nashville, Tenn.  Jesse Hail, Grant No.
19444,.for 50 acres.Oct.26- 1835 Book 19 page 332.
Jesse W. Hail Grant No. 18109. for 90 acres dated Oct.13- 1833. Book 18 page
156.
Lewis Hale Grant No. 17607 for 120 acres. Dated Aug. 29- 1832 Book 17, page 460.
Hugh D. Hale, Grant No. 22633. for 40 acres dated Aug. 26- 1839 Book 22, page
385.
Hugh D. Hale, Grant No. 3765 for 5 acres dated April 20- 1816 Book 4 page 337.
Joseph Hale, grant No. 29905 dated June 8- 1857 Book 30 page 635.
Meshack Halo, Grant No.6402. for 50 acres, Dated Dec. 10- 1819, Book 6 page 62.
P.H. Hale, Grant No. 21023, for 20 acres dated July 20- 1837 Book 21 page 31.

Mashack Hail, will. March 20-1834. Green County, named wife Mary, children
Lewis,Nancy, Charles, Enoch, Sarah, Mary, Jackson, James, Elijah,  proved 1834.

Administrators Bond for estate of Meshack Haile --- Mary Haile and Lewis Hale and
Enoch Hail with James Haws as surety. -- 1832. ( In Old will care in Letter H).

Deed of Trust Book # 2 (Old Book). page 20. Enoch Halo to Elijah Hale certain
property from the estate of Charles Hale decd. Jany 1842.

Elijah Hail conveys to Lewis Hail certain peoperty in Trust deed. Book 2. page
238 Green Co.

Deed Book 31 page 14. William Nelson and Harriet Nelson formerly Harriet Hale
to Mary A. Hale  a lot of ground which her ( Harriott's)father  Joshua Hale died
seized of. April 30- 1860.

Catherine Jane Hale to Christopher Haun 2 tracts of land. Catherine recites her-
self as of Franklin County Tenn. She transfers her right to Sydnah Hale, James
R. Hale, and Alexander W. Halo. June 13- 1851 ( Deed Book 26 page 88).

Deed of Trust from Elijah Hale to Lewis Hale to secure payment of debt. Jany
27- 1849. ( Greenville, Tenn. Green Co. Book 23, page 317.).

Philip S. Hale of Hawkins Co. born Dec. 10- 1830 son of Philip S. and Elizabeth
(Bachman) Hale. The father a native of Greene County and the mother of Sullivan
County. They married in Sullivan County and lived at Kingsport a while and had
12 children. ( Goodspeed's History of East Tenn. page 1228-9).

Marriages in Greene County Tenn. -- John Hail and Sarah Lauderdale Oct.19-1801.
              Thomas L. Hale and Eliza W. Porter  March 19- 1817 surety H.D.Hale.
              Booker B. Hale and Nancy Pearce Jan. 23- 1834.
              John Hale and Jane Cimery July 31- 1829
              Amon Hail to Susannah Hail Jany 25-1806 surety Achillis Hail.
              Jinny Hail and John Dittamore Dec. 5- 1810 surety Frederick Hail,
              John Hale and Anny Brown April 5- 1824.
              Endimyon Hale and Sarah Hale Jany 10-1824.
              William Gibson and Margarat Hale  Nov, 16- 1799 surety Frederick Hale.
              David M. Dobson and Nancy Halo  Jany 31-1832,
               William Neilson and Sarah Hale. Dec. 31- 1801 surety Wm. Halo.
              Charles F. Keith and Eliza D. Hale Oct. 30- 1811.
              Abner Hope and Margaret Hale Sept.19-1827
              Chas. T.J. Jarnagin and Catherine Ann Hale Aug. 26-1834.
              Christian Hale  and Polly Bible Jany 2- 1811.
              James Scruggs and Catherine H. Halo Sept. 23- 1823,
              Jacob Halo and Catherine King, March 26, 1821.

32

David Lackland and Elizabeth Hale, March 15, 1820.
Joseph Hale and Peggy Buster Feby 6- 1816.
George Hale and Elizabeth Buster Oct. 7-1818.
Robert Magill and Polly Hail Aug. 1- 1808.
William Hale and Betsy Lackland Aug. 9- 1808
Bird B. Hail and Nancy Lackey, Dec. 12- 1808 surety Amon Hail and
                                        Evan Evans Sr.
John Miller and Peggy Hale Dec. 13- 1826.
Stephen King and Nancy Hale Oct. 17- 1826.
Hervey Hail and Esther Brotherton Nov. 12- 1816.

*********************************************************
---------------------------------------------------------------------

HALE FAMILY NOTES FROM HAWKINS COUNTY TENNESSEE RECORDS

In the U.S. Census of 1830 Washington D.C. I have made note on the following--
Solomon Hale, Philip S. Hale, George Hale with families living in that year.

George Hale was a member of the first grand jury in Hawkins County in 1810.
( Goodspeed's History of East Tennessee. page 875).

A petition to the Legislature of Tenn, asking for about 140 indictments against
certain citizens for betting on horse races be annulled. The signers included
Tunnid Hale and Geo. Hale. ( Legislative papers State Archives, Nashville Box.
82.).

Alexander Hale aged 33 years born in Tennessee in 1850 census. In same house
Penelope Hale aged 30 years and Elizabeth Hale aged 21 years all born in Tenn.
(U.S. Census report 1850. Washington D.C.).

Wesley A. Phipps married Eliza Hale of Hawkins Co. Wesley was born Sept. 16,
1816 died 1882. Eliza was born about 1820 and died 1865. ( Goodspeed's History
of East Tenn. page 1235).

Hannah Hale married Jas. Lee. He was born in Hawkins County 1786 and died 1866.
James Lee was son of Thomas Lee of Virginia. ( Goodspeed's History of East
Tenn. page 1231).

Jesse Hale's will in Book 1869 page 95. mentions wife Harriet Hale, son James
M. Hale, Wm. A. Hale, daughter Mary E. C. Hale and daughter Lovinia J. Hale.

Ogden Hale's will. in will book 1797-1884. page 253. dated Dec. 13,1841 proved
1848. mentions daughter Anna Kelly, son Harbey Hale, son Thomas Hale, son
Arthur Hale, son Jesse Hale, son Turner Hale, daughter Kiziah Hale, son Samuel
Hale and wife Lovina Hale.

Arthur Hale's Will. same book as above page 255. wife Jane. two oldest daus.
land adj. Barnabas Kelly and David Tates to be divided equally between Hiley J.
and Betsy Viney Hale. To son Kindred Hale . dated 1845 proved 1847. Mentions
also Alice and Martha Hale.

Canida Hale aged 35 a female born in Tennessee is shown in census of 1850
and with her a William Hale aged 12 years, Elizabeth Hale aged 10 years and
Isaac Hale aged 8 months, all born in Tennessee. ( U.S. Census 1850 Washington)

33

P. Smith Hale aged 57 years a farmer in Hawkins County Census report of 1850.
He was born in Tennessee. In the same house lived Elizabeth Hale aged 52, born
in Tennessee, Philip Hale a laborer aged 19 years, William Hale aged 17 years,
also a laborer, Mary Hale aged 15 years, Frances Hale aged 13 years, Adelaida
Hale, aged 10 years, Josephine Hale aged 9 years, and Ellen Hale aged 7 years,
all born in Tennessee. ( U.S. Census Report 1850 Washington D.C.).

Legislative Petition for the annexation of Hawkins Co. Tenn. 1851 signed by
a number including Thomas Hale. ( Box 84 Tenn. State Archives).

Nancy Flora widow of Daniel Flora asking for benefit of certain land warrant.
Nov. 1- 1843 to this petition to the Legislation of Tenn. is the name of
George Hale ( Legislative Petitions Tenn. State Archives Box. 91).

## SOME HALE FAMILY NOTES FROM SULLIVAN COUNTY TENNESSEE

In 1840 census I have noted  David Bragg ( father-in-law of Lewis Hale(E.R.W)),
Lewis Hale, Jeremiah Hale  and others will be found. ( Census report 1840, Washington D.C.).

Thomas Titsworth married Nancy Hale the daughter of Lewis Hale and Elizabeth
Bragg, his first wife.  (E.R.W.).

Crawford Hale aged 42 years a lawyer in the census of 1850. Born in Kentucky.
Had in his house Rebecca H. E (C) Hale aged 40 years born in Virginia, Caroline
F. Hale aged 13 years and Augusta V. Hale, aged 6 years. ( U.S. Census report
1850 Washington. )

The first Baptist Society in the county was formed at Kendricks Creek Church
and it was organized by Jonathan Mulkey prior to 1786. Among the first members
was Nicholas Hale. ( Goodspeed's History of East Tenn. 1887. page 914).

Lilburn Hale dec'd heirs by attorney & c, To Joseph Henry. deed. Dist. 15, 100
acres Book 31 page 355. March 19-1881. Recorded Dec. 20-1881. This is the
sale of certain property inherited from their mother Elizabeth Bragg Hale the
first wife of Lewis Hale. It mentions. We Charles Hale in his own right and
as attorney in fact for Nancy Titsworth and her husband Thomas Titsworth, Lewis
Hale, James H. Hale, Elijah Hale, David B. Halo, and the heirs of Lilburn Hale
deceased to wit-- James C. Hale, Lewis Hale, Nancy A. Ridge and her husband
Joseph Ridge and Lilburn S. Hale ·and also for ourselves we Enoch K. Hale and
wife Mary Hale and Elizabeth Hale for and in consideration of the sum of five
hundred dollars to,us in hand paid have this day bargained and sold by these
presents do bargain sell transfer and convey to Joseph F. Henry  a tract of land.
( Sullivan County Tenn. records at Blountville.).

In deed Book 26 page 134-135 same place as above " Know all men by these present
to that we Lewis Hale of the County of Scott and Meshack Hale and Nancy Titsworth
formerly Nancy Hale with her husband Thomas Titsworth who joins with her in this
instrument of the County of Schuyler in the State of Missouri and James C. Hale,
Lewis Hale, Lilburn S. Hale, and Nancy A. Ridge who join with her in the
execution of this instrument all of the County of Shelby in the said state of
Missouri" The said last four being the heirs at law of Lilburn Hale late of
the County of Shelby deceased, and all being of full age." And James H. Hale
of Greene Co. State of Illinois, and David B.Hale of the County of Harrison in
the State of Texas and Elijah H. Hale of the County of Hunt in the State of Texas,

34

they with one Charles Hale hereinafter mentioned being all the heirs of one
Elizabeth Hale deceased lately of the County of Sullivan and state of Tennessee
and wife of one Lewis Hale now of said County have made constituted and appointed
and by these presents do make constitute and appoint the said Charles Hale of
the said County of Schuyler in the said State of Missouri our true "and lawful
attorney" to dispose of certain property in Sullivan County, Tenn, that the said
Elizabeth Hale died seized and possed of at her death, especially the property
she inherited from one David Bragg, after the death of Elizabeth Bragg the wife
of the said David by his last will and testament 13 day of May 1830. etc.

Will of David Bragg of Sullivan County, Tenn. ( Original on file in Blountville
Tenn)-- mentions wife Elizabeth Bragg, Anna Pickens and Elizabeth Hale. Calls
them both his daughters. Mentions his former daughter-in-law the wife of son
who is now dead, and now Mary Jolly one dollar. Dated May 13-1834. Proved June
3-1844. witnessed by Thomas Murrell, John Peoples Jr., and N. W. Bachman.

Lewis Hale's Will on file in Sullivan County Tenn, at Blountville. (Original
will). Mentions wife Elizabeth Hale, son William W. Hale, son Enoch, and son
Elijah to have fifty dollars each, mentions balance of heirs but not by name.
( did not leave balance of heirs any property). Makes wife Elizabeth and William
S. White Executors. Feb. 27, 1874. witnessed by Adam S. Branes, George R. Barnes,
and proved in Sullivan County Oct. 4- 1860. Recorded in Will book page 344.

Lewis Hale received grant of land no. 27818 for 412 acres Oct. 22- 1850 in
Sullivan County ( Land Office Nashville Tenn.).

Phillip S. Hale received Grant No.11704, for 200 acres dated Aug. 27- 1825
Book 10 page 751 ( Land Office Nashville).

Lewis Hale received grant No. 28041 for 503 acres dated July 30- 1851 recorded
Book 28 page 1169 ( Land Office Nashville).        2016539

Some Deeds in Sullivan County:
          Robert G. Hale and Sarah & c.to Robert Trebute. Tr. Kindrix Creek
Book 11 page 19 deed Oct. 22- 1827.
          Stephen Hale from Martha DeVault one negro  Book 12 page 141 Bill of
Sale Feb. 1-1838.
          Lewis Hale from Elizabeth Bragg 2 negroes  Book 13, page 276 Bill of
Sale, July 23-1842.
          Lewis Hale to Shadrack J. Murrell-- Boundary Line, Book 16, page 234.
Bond. Mar. 27, 1850. Agreement.
          Lydia J. Hail to Martin Jones, Book 16, page 270 power of attorney
Oct. 8, 1850.
          Lewis Hail & c. to James Pickens Jr. -- Tr. Straight Creek.-- Book
16 page 424 deed Oct. 2- 1848.
          Lewis Hale from Elizabeth Bragg Book 14 page 244 Agreement. Sept. 1-
1844.
          Lewis Hail from Wm. Pickens & c. 19¾ acres Horse Creek  Book 16,page
110 deed Oct. 20, 1849.
          Lewis Hail from Michael Mullen, ½ acre Horse Creek. Book 19 page 250
deed May 17, 1856.
          Enoch R. Hale from Lewis Hale 56 acres Horse Creek ( and Personal
Property) Book 22 page 329 deed May 4, 1859.
          Lewis Hail from State of Tennessee 503 acres Horse Creek. Book 17,
page 236. Grant July 30- 1851.
          Lewis Hale to Michael Mullens 3 acres Horse Creek Book 19 page 101
deed May 17, 1856.
          Lewis Haile from Michael Mullens and Nancy 3 acres Horse Creek. Book

19, page 249 deed, May 17-1856.
Enoch K. Hale from J.F. Howard and Eliza A. Book 23 page 343. Power
of attorney Sept. 1-1877.
Landen C. and Aniser B. Hale to Jesse C. Yoaksley interest in 128
acres Book. 25 page 390 deed. Sept. 2- 1873.
Alexander Hale from John Ford, 100 acres Book 2 page 788 deed Feb.
23, 1795.
Samuel Hale from Thomas Vincent. 200 acres on Horse Creek, Book 5,
page 200. deed Aug. 13- 1808.
George Hale from David Ross , Doc. by Ex. Lot No. 44. Rossville.
Book 7 page 376 deed Nov. 7, 1818.
Phillip S. Hale from George Morrison negro woman and child Book 9
page 379 Bill of Sale March 25, 1822.
John Hale from North Carolina 600 acres Bent Creek Book 1. page
75. Aug. 18, 1783.
John Hail from North Carolina 200 acres Honeycuts Creek. Book 1.
page 116 Aug. 18-1783.
Alexander Hale and Sarah from John Billingsley 112 acres Sinking
Creek Book 2 page 787. Gift for love and affection. Feb. 23-1795 May 23-1795.

************************************
----------------------------------------------------------------

LIST WAR OF 1812 SOLDIERS AS RECORDED IN THE FILES
OF THE TENNESSEE STATE LIBRARY
NASHVILLE TENNESSEE.

By name Hail,Hale.

George Hale No. 283 Colonel Feby. 29, 1813 from Hawkins County. served 4th Regi
John Hale No. 286 Lieutenant. Oct.27-1813 Hawkins Co. 4th Regiment.
Nicholas Hail, Ensign Jan. 31-1814 Jackson County, Tenn. 48th Regiment.
Butler Hail, Capt. May 21-1815, Giles County, Tenn. 2nd Regiment.
Jobe Hail, Lieutenant, July 17-1815 Hickman Co. 36th Regiment.

| PRIVATES | | PRIVATES |
|---|---|---|
| Hale, Alexander | Hale, Wilson | Hail, Nicholas |
| , Bird | Haile, Chase | , Richard |
| ,Dickerson | , George | , Sherwood |
| , Ezekial | , Hezekiah | , Thos |
| , George | , Jesse | ;William |
| , Hugh | , Leroy | |
| , James | , Nicholas | |
| , Jesse | ,'Richard | NOTE: Reports on these |
| , John | , Samuel | men may be had either |
| , Joseph | , Walter | from Washington D.C. |
| , Lemon | Hailes,Daniel | War department or from |
| , Leroy | Hail, Alexander | research in the Tennessee |
| , Mashack | , Christopher | State Library. E.R.W. |
| , Micajah | , Ezekial | |
| , Nathan G, | , George | |
| , Nicholas | , Gillilard | |
| , Richard | Hail(Hale)Jeremiah | |
| , Samuel | Hail, Jesse | |
| , Sherwood | , John A. | |
| , Talbot | , John B. | |
| , Thomas | , Leo Roy | |
| , Waller | , Massack | |
| , William | , Micaja | |

Carter County, Tenn. Deed Book A. page 43. 7 day Sept. 1796 John Hails of
Carter County from Samuel Gerlard 50 pounds. Land in Limestone Cove, adjoining
James Stuart's line containing 50 acres. Witness--- Gutradg Garland, James
Tate (Tater), Charles Coyler. Registered Jan. 19-1797.

Carter County. Tenn. Book A. page 44. Sept.13- 1796. John Hale of Carter Co. to
William King of Sullivan County 100 dollars sell said ½m. King in trust for and
to the use benefit and behoof of Jonathan King a minor nephew to the said William King a certain piece or parcel of land part of said John Hale's plantation
situate, lying and being in Carter County. On bank of river Watauga at Bogarts
corner. containing 160 acres. Signed John Hale, Reg. Jany 19-1797.

Carter County, Tenn. Book. A. page 135. 29 Dec. 1797 John Hale of Carter County
to John Lacy 200 pounds a tract of land 189 acres in Carter County on Lick Creek
adjoining King's line signed John Hale. Witnessed by John Carter, Armstead Blevins,
and E. Folson. Registered Jany 16- 1798.

Carter County Tenn. Deed Book G. page 80. -- Ann Hale of Carter County, bind unto
Samuel Smithson her son William Henry aged 4 years until he arrives at age of
21 years. Condition that Smithson bind himself to furnish the boy with home
and comfortable board, clothes etc and agrees to give him two years schooling
etc. Jany 20- 1839 proved in court Nov. 27- 1839.

James L. Hail to N. A. Williams Oct. 21- 1825. Carter County. Marriage.

Hyram Hale ( Hall) to Nancy Ballard . marriage Sept. 26-1850 . Carter County.

Blount County Tenn. --- Jake and Thomas Hail Grant No. 1362 for 315 acres
dated May 26, 1810 book 2-1 page 486 Tennessee State Land Office, Nashville.

Blount County, Tenn. ---- Thomas Hail grant No.1362 for 315 acres dated May 26-
1810 Book 2-1 page 465 ( Tenn Land Records Nashville).

Blount County, Tenn. Thomas Hail to Rosanna Denno. April 23-1801 ( surety
Luke Hail) marriage.

Blount County, Tenn. Sarah Hail to Samuel Torry. marriage Oct. 3-1797.

A petition on file in the Legislative Papers from Jefferson County Tenn. Box. 4.
Tenn. State Archives at Nashville. This petition. is one asking that no new
county be made within certain bounds. dated 1801. Among the names attached thereto are Job Haile and Joseph Hale.

Monroe County, Tenn. Stephen P. Hale, born in McMinn County near Athens, Nov.
1-1825 son of William and Sarah (Porter) Hale. The father was born in Grayson
County Virginia Jany 11- 1802 and died in Monroe County Tenn. 2/21/1845.
( Goodspeed's History of East Tenn. page 999).

Davidson County Tenn. Marriages--- William Hale and Sally Brown March 18-1799.

Bedford County, Tenn. Grants, Land Office Nashville -- Entry 135. Meshack Haile
Grant No. 3063 for 100 acres May 6-1826.

Smith County, Tenn.   Deeds of 1833. -- Jacob Hale to Joseph Hale page 234.
also, Joab Hale from James McCormack, page 243.

Smith County, Tenn.----- Deed Book D. page 265. ----- Leeman Hale of Smith County
deed to his beloved children, William H. Hale, Sarah W. Hale, Thomas J. Hale,
Martha E. Hale and Dudley E. Hale and because the said Leeman Hale is moving.
Sept. 1-1813.

Susan Hale married Jacob Range. Their daughter Eliza A. married Samuel H. Miller
1840. Susan Hale Range died aged 73 years and Jacob Range at 87 years.  (Goodspeed's History of East Tenn. Washington Co. page 1279).

Jackson County, Tennessee ---- Legislative petition to General Assembly of Tenn.
filed Box. 75 State Archives, Nashville. regarding a new county dated 1837
and among those signing said petition I find -----( all signers from western
part of Jackson and Smith counties and the signers are those in favor of the
division of the county) ---- Luke Hail .

One Hale family in Rutherford and Bedford Counties as early as 1840, lived
near the county line  not far from the settlement called Deason. (E.R.W.)
This is not far from Fosterville. (E.R.W) This family inter-married with the
Odom, Thompson, Miller  and one Will Hale married the widow Green and lived
about three miles from Christiana in Rutherford County, Tenn. ( E.R.W.).

*********************
*********************
*********************

38

Hale, Alfred. 31.
  Alexander. 26.27.30.
    31.33.36.
  Alexander W. 32.
  Alice. 33.
  Alison(Allison) 22.
    27.29.31.
  Allen. D. 30.
  Amon.20.21.22.23.
    27.32.33.
  Andrew. J. 25.
  Aniser.B. 36.
  Anna. 26.
  Annaliza. 23.
  Anne. 10.11.12.28.
    29.37.
  Archibald. 22.26.
    27.29.31.
  Armstrong. 3.
  Arthur. 33.
  Augusta V. 34.
  Benjamine.3.28.
  Betsy. 5. 12.
  Betsy Viney.33.
  Booker. B. 32.
  Burd (Bird) B.27.
    30.33.36.
  Burd. 26.
  Caleb. 2.
  Canday. 28.
  Canida. 33.
  Carmilita. 18.
  Caroline. F. 34.
  Caroline S. 26.
  Casandra. 12.
  Catherine. 10.31.
  Catherine Ann. 32.
  Catherine D. 31.
  Catherine H. 32.
  Catherine Jane. 32.
  Charity. 11.
  Charlie. M. 18.
  Charles 6.18.22.27.
    31.32.34.35.
  Charley. 18.
  Chase. 22. 23. 27.
    38.
  Cheneth. 23.
  Chenoth. 22.
  Chinowth. 18.25.28.
  Christian.31.32.
  Clary. 28.
  Clauda. 27.
  Crawford. 34.
  Daniel. 10.25.
  David. 14.18.26.29.
  David B. 26.34.
  Deborah. 18.
  Delsenah. 20.
  Dickerson. 36

Hale, Dorcus. 28.
  D. Maliday. 28.
  Dudley. 38.
  E.B. 25.
  Edmond. 22.
  E. D. 18.
  Edward. 2.3.5.6.10.
  Elanor. 28.
  Elbert Dewit. 18
  Eleart 28.
  Elias. 12.
  Elijah. 18.28.30.32.34.
    35.
  Elijah H. 34.
  Elizabeth.3.14.18.20.23.
    25.26.27.28.29.33.
    .34.35.
  Elizabeth Bragg. 34.
  Eliza D. 32.
  Wliza 25.26.33.
  Eliza M. 26.
  Ellen. 34.
  Elmira (Beacon).25.
  Emalene. 29.
  Emma Kiser. 20.
  Emma Sue. 18.
  Endimyon. 32.
  Enoch. 18.19.21.22.23.26.
    30.32.35.
  Enoch K. 34.36.
  Enoch. R. 35.
  Ezekial. 36.
  F. D. 28.
  Fereby. 14.
  Finley. 27,28.29.
  Franklin. 31.
  Franklin D. 28.29
  Frederick (Frederick)19.
    32.
  Fuller. P. 18.
  Garland. B. 13.
  Gentry. 18.
  George.1.6.22.23.28.29.
    31.33.34.36.
  George B. 23. 24. 27.
  George S. 23.26.31.
  George T. 25.
  George W. 25.
  Guy. 26.
  Hannah. 3.12. 26. 28. 33.
  Hannah. Ellis. 20.
  Hannah. Ligon. 29.
  Harbey. 33.
  Harriet. 25.28,29.31.
    32.33.
  Harrison. 26.
  Harvey. N. 28.
  Henry. 22. 23.25.26.27.
    28.29.
  Hezekiah. 21.

Hale, Hiley J. 33.
  Hiram. D. 23.28.29.
  Hubbard. 28.
  Hugh. 31.36.
  Hugh. D. 29.30.31.32
  Hutts. 26.
  H. D. 32.
  Hyram. 37.
  Isaac. 12.33.
  Isabella.G. 26.
  Isabella. 28.
  Isham. 3. 16.
  J. 27.
  Jacob. 32. 38.
  Jack. 22.
  Jackson. 26.28.32.
  J.C. 25.
  James.3.12.18.22.23.
    24.26.29.31.32.
    36.
  James Bible. 31.
  James C. 23.30.34.
  James. E. 20.23.26.
    30.
  James Edmundson.3.
  James Ellis. 26.
  James F. 25.
  James H. 34.
  James J. 18.
  James Lewis. 3.
  James. M. 33.
  James R. 32.
  J. H. 26.
  Jane. 3.9.12.28.33.
  Jeese. 26.33.
  Jeremiah.26.27.34.
  Jesse. 12.13.14.20.
    32.36.
  Jesse. W. 30.32.
  Jimmy. J. 18.
  Jinny. 32.
  Joab. 38.
  Jobe. 12.
  John. 1.3.5.6.7.10.
    12.14.18.19.21.22.
    24.25.26.27.28.29.
    30.31.32.36.37.
  John A. C. 25.
  John B. 29.30.
  John C. 27.
  Mrs. John. E. 22.
  Johhny. 12.
  Jonah. 5.
  Jonas. 14.
  Jordan Elbert. 28.
  Josephine 34.
  Joseph. 3.5.12.13.19
    21.22.23.26.27.28
    29.30.31.32.33.36.
    37.38.

Hale, Joseph Fuller.18;
  Joseph L. 25.28.29.
  Joshua.12.20.22.
    29.31.32.
  Joshua S. 29.
  Josiah. 14.
  Keziah. M. 3.
  Killns. 30.
  Kindred. 33.
  Kiziah. 33.
  Landon Carter.20.
    26.27.28.36.
  Laura 26.
  Lavinia. J. 33.
  Leoman. 38.
  Lemon. 36.
  Leonard. 4.
  Leroy. 21.22.27.36.
  Lewis. 5.7.15.18.
    19.22.23.24.26.
    32.34.35.
  Lilburn. 15.22.34.
  Lilburn S. 34.
  Louisa. 28.
  Lovina. 33.
  Lucy. 28.
  Lucinda. 29.
  Mancroce. 25.
  Margaret, 32.
  Mark. 18.19.22.23.
    26.27.
  Martha. 25. 28.29.
    33.
  Martha.E. '38.
  Mary.2.3.7.12.15.
    20.22.23.24.25.
    26.29.30.32.34.
  Mary. A. 32. 34.
  Mary.E. C. 33.
  Mary Jane.28.
  Matilda Elizabeth.
    26.
  Matthew. 14.
  Maxey. 3.
  Meade. 5.
  Menirva. 31.
  Merah. 23.
  Messack. 23.24.
  Moshack.15.18.21.
    22.23.26.27.28.
    30.32.34.36.
  Micajah. 20.36.
  Molly. M. 20.
  Nancy.2.3.6.12.18.
    26.27.28.32.33.
    34.
  Nancy A. 34.
  Nancy Ann. 15.
  Nancy Ruth. 18.

Hale, Nathan.14.20.21.27.
  Nathan.C. 36.
  Nathaniel. 31.
  Ned. 22.
  Nicholas. 11.16.18.20.
    21.26.27.29.34.
  Ogden.33.
  Crlena. 13.18.
  P.H.32,
  Patrick. H. 31.
  P. P. 26.
  Patty. 3,
  Peggy. 33.
  Penelope. 33.
  Peter. 3.
  Philip 31.34.
  Philip S. 31.32.33.35.
    36.
  Phillip. 29.
  Polly.14.23.26.
  Pool.6.
  Preston. 3.
  Prisse. 20.
  P. Smith. 34.
  Rachel. 3.
  Rebecca. 31.
  Rebecca H.E. 34
  Rena. 28.
  Rhoda Glen. 18.
  Richard.3.6.18.20.21.
    24.26.28.36.
  Robert.G. 20.22.35,
  R. L. 18.
  Rufus. 3.
  Ruth. 12.19.20.26.27.
  Sabrina. 18.
  Sallie.E. 20.
  Sally. 12.
  Sam. 26.
  Samuel.10.12.20.27.28.
    29.31.33.36.
  Sarah.3.18.23.25.26.27.
    28.31.32.35.36.37.
  Sarah W. 38.
  Seaby. 3.
  Shadrack.15.21.22.23.
    24.25.27.
  Shadrack. G. 20.
  Sherwood. 36.
  Smith. H. 28.29.
  Solomon. 26.33.
  Stephen. 3. 26.35.
  Stephen.P.37.
  Stephensnd.3.
  Susannah.3.18.29.32.
  Susan.28.38.
  Susan Emma. 18.
  Sydnah.32.
  Talbot. 36.

Hale, Temperance. 24,25.
  Thomas.2.3.6.10.12.
    20,22,25,27,28.,
    33.34.36.
  Thomas J. 38.
  Thomas L. 30.31.32.
  Thomas S. 28.
  Tom. 26.
  Tunnid. 33.
  Turner. 33.
  Uratha.20.
  Virginia E. 18.
  Waller. 36.
  Walter. 19.
  Walter Burson. 18.
  W. B. 3.
  W. C. 25.
  Wm. C. 29.
  Wicks. 3.
  William.j.3.4.6.12.
    14.15.19.20.22.26.
    27.28.29.31.33.34.
    36.37.
  Will. 38.
  William A. 33.
  William C. 20.
  William H. 38.
  William W. 35.
  Wilson. 36.
  Zachariah. 22.27.28.
Hales, George 6,
  Isaiah.15.
  John.6.
  Joyce. 1.
  Lewis. 11.
  Miss ___ 6.
  Nathaniel. 5.
  Silas. 11.
  Will. 6.
Hayle, Barbara 2.
  Chapman. 15.
  Nicholas.2.7.9.
  Thomas. 2.
Hayles,Daniel.14.
  Hosey. 14.
  James. 14.
  Joe.14
  Jonas. 14.
  Joseph. 14.
  Joshua. 14.
Heale. Allison. 28.
  Ellen. 1.
  Elizabeth. 1.
  Frances 1.
  George. 1.2.4.
  Hannah. 1.
  John1.
  Joseph. 1.
  Nathaniel.2.

Heale, Nicholas. 1.2.     Heale, Symon. 2.
     Richard. 2.        William. 1.2.
     Sarah. 1.       Hoyle, Edward. 4.
     Simson. 2.

-----------------------------------------------------

# INDEX
(Persons named other than
Hale, Hail, Haile, Heale,)

Mary. 18.24.
Orvil. 26.
Sally. 28,
Coyler, Charles. 27.
Craghead. Ann. 3.
Dicey. 3.
Jenny. 3.
John. 3.
Craighead, John. 3.
Craine, Maria. 6.
Crocketts, David.19.
William. 19.
Curtis, Fannie. 28.
Dabney, Charles. 5.
Davenport, William. 1.
David, Elizabeth. 11.
Davis, Henry. 2.5.
Dawson, David. 11.
Day, Mary. 7. 11.
Decine, Elizabeth. 12.
Denne, Rosanna. 37.
Devine, David. 12.
DeVault. Martha. 35.
Dhickerson, John.10.
Dickerson, Charlotte. 3.
Risamond.10.
Dittamore, John. 32.
Dobson, David. M. 32.
Donelson, John. 5.
Doney ( Dowey) Anthony. 2.
Dooney, Daniel. 12.
Dott, John. 29.
Dotson.William. 27.
Douglas, Catherine. 31.
Mary. 28.
Duncan. Joseph. 19.
Durham, Charles, 21.
Duncan, Thelma. 29.
Early, Jerh. 10.
Eddlemons, Michael. 21.
Edmundson, Humphrey, 9
Richard. 9.
Elberry, William. 2.
Elks, Richard. 14.
Ellis, Hannah, 26.
Embree, Elisha. 19.
Evans, Evan, 33.
Everett, Simonds, 9.
Fauntleroy, Moore, 1.
Ferguson. Kate.6.
Miss. ___ 26
Fields, Lieut. John. 25.
Finnie (Finney) Peter.9.
Fitzgerald, Aiken. 27
12.
Flora. Daniel. 34.
Nancy. 34.
Flovell, William. 14.

Ford, (Foard) John. 36.
Loyd. 21
Thomas 16.
Folson, E. 37.
Fox, William. 1.
Frankling, Dicey. 3.
Franklin, Samuel. 28.
Fulwider, Jim, 19.
Gaines, Bed 9
Galloway, ___ 22.
Garland, Gutrndg, 37.
Gerland, Samuel. 37.
Geovers, George. 19.
Gibson, Archbell, 10.
Catherine. 4.
James. 4. 10.
John. 10.
Joseph. 10.
Randell.10.
William. 19. 32.
Gillespie. Allen. 29.
Good. R. 27.
Gose, Nancy. 10.
Gray. James. 29.
Jane., 19
Nathan. 30
Sarah. 20
Grays, Jim. 18.
Green, Ralph. 2.
___ 38
Gresham, Elizabeth. 28.
George. 29
Thomas 28
Grimmett, Solomon. 3.
Gulley, Lazaras. 19.
Guess, Nancy. 28.
Hair, Asa. 28.
John. 23.
Hall, A. M. 30.
James. 30.
William. 1.
Hanna. James. 12.
Hatcher, Sarah. 9.
Wm. 3
Haun, Christopher, 32.
Hawes, Phoebe. 19
Haws, Thos. 19.
Hawker (Howker) Enoch. 2.
Hawley, James. 2.
Haws, James. 23, 27, 30, 32.
Nancy. 23.
Hay, Felix, 12.
Gilbert. 12.
Heabord, John.1.
William. 1.
Heath. William. 9.
Henderson, William. Henry.23
Henry. Joseph. 34.

Joseph F. 34.
William. 37.
Hill, Isaac. 14.
Hiller, A. D. 20.
Hilton, Marrek. 19
Hilton, Marrek. 19
Hinkle, Margaret.28
Hipinstate, Joseph. 17.
Hitchcock, 11.
Hodges, Robert. 3.
Hope, Abner. 32.
Hopper, ___ 23.
Horton, Isaac. 27.
Howar,Elisa A. 24.
Howard, Eliza A. 36.
Joseph. 23.
J. F. 36.
Howell, Elizabeth. 5.
Hough, Daniel. 3.
Hubbard, Lydia A. 26
Hubberd, Ann. 2.
Hulse,J. V. 24
Hunt, Jesse. 16.
Martha. 29.
Uriah. 26.
Huzzey, Elijah. 16.
Hynds, Mary. L. 18.
Ingram, Thomas 19
William. 19.
Jackson, Betsy. 5.
General. 31.
George 21.31
John W. 28
Margaret. 28
Martha. 28
Polly. 12
Polly Ann. 28
William. 21
Janey, Jno. 2.
Jarnagin, Chas. T. J. 32.
Jenkins, Howell, 29.
Johnson, Laranza D. 10.
Marke. 2.
Jolly, Mary. 35.
Jones, Abraham. 27.
Jesse. 3.
Martha. 35.
Matilda. 3
Nancy. J. 31
Tabitha 3.
Jordan. Hannah. 28.
Keith. Charles. F. 32.
Elizabeth. D. 31
Kellam, John 11.
Kelly, Ann. 33.
Barnabas 33
Wm. 12
Kennedy, Jane. 27.
John. 19.

Kincheloe, Elizabeth 27.
John. 25.
Mary. 15.18.
Kincholow, Harriet. 19.
Margaret. 29.
Kinhard, William. 19.
Killingdworth, Jeremiah.
19.
King,Catherine, 32.
Elix F. 30
Jonathan. 37
Mary. 6.
Mr.___ 26
William. 37.
Stephen. 33.
Kinser, Rev. P. P.18
Kizer, Emy. 26.
Lackland, David. 33.
Patsy. 33
Lackey, Nancy. 33.
Lacy. John. 37.
Landers, Capt. James. 24
Landon, James. 18.
Landrum, Rebecca. C. 31.
Lauderdale, Sarah. 32.
Lawson,Catherine. 30
Lee, Kendall. 1.
Micajah. 19.
Thomas 19. 33.
Long, Richard. H. 12.
William. 12.
Lucas. John 29.
McAddams, Ibby. 19
McCloud, Mary. 3.
McCormack, James. 38.
McCown, Mary. 24.
McCrary.Elizabeth. 18.
McCubbins, Zachariah. 16
McNamee, Peter. 17.
McPike, William. 22.
Magill, Robert. 33.
Majors, Henderick, 31.
Marshall,Frances H. 23.
John 14.
Joseph. 23.
Massongill, Deborah. 18.
Matlock, Barbara 28
Isham. 28.
Nancy. 28.
Ransom. 28.
Mattox, David. 3.
Matthew, Jonathan. 16.
Mays, John 12.
Maxoy. Suckey. 5.
Mead. Wm. 9.
Melvanos, Capt. 24
Metcalf. Ann. 1.
Miles, Will. 2.
Miller, Elizabeth. 6.

James. 21.
John. 33.
Samuel H. 38
Millet, G. W. 22
Millward, James. 7.
Mitchell, John. 19.
Richard. 19.
Ruth. 19.
Moody, William. 5.
Moodoy, Jonny. 5.
Moore, James, 27.
John. 17
Mary Ann. 24.
Morgan, Capt. Frances. 2.
Morgin, Thomas 9
William.9
Morris, Sarah. 3.
Zekel. 3.
Morrison, George. 36
Morrow, Malinda. 31.
Muligans, John 12
Mulkey, Jonathan. 34.
Mullen, Michael.35
Mureys, Capt. 24.25.
Murpheys, 7.
Murrays, Thomas 21.
Murrell, Richard. 18
Shadrack, J. 35.
Thomas 35.
Neilson, Sarah. 31
William. 32.
Nelson,George. 19.
Harriet. 32
William. 32.
Nuckolls, Ezca (Zra) 3.4.
Odel, Mollie. 25.
Odom, ___ 38.
Ogletree, Nancy. 12.
Opie, John 1.
Lindsey. 1.
Overstreet, ___ 79.
Paine, Wm. 19.
Pate,Mrs. ___ 26.
Payne, Susanna. 6.
Pearce, Nancy. 32.
Phillip. G. 27.
Peoples, John. 35.
Perdue, Patsy,2
Poteet, Joe. 22.
Peyton, Frances 12.
Phelps, John. 7.
Pherson, Ellen. 28.
Phipps. Wesley. A. 33.
Pickens, Anna. 35.
James. 35.
Wm. 35.
Plue, Polly. 12.
Poindexter, James. 26.
Pollack, Thomas. 14.

Poll. Minetrea. 3.
Porter, Eliza W. 32
Thos. 3.
Pratt, John. 5.
Pritchett, Amanda. Jane.
29.
Quarles, John. 9.
Qusenberry, ___ 8.
Range, Eliza A. 38.
Jacob. 38
Ranger, James C. 24.
Rassieur, Hassie. 24.
Raves, Moses, 19
Rees, James. 6.
Register, Julia. 26
Ennick, Samuel.12.
Rentfro. William. 9.10
Rice, Catherine Dorothy
12
Elizabeth 12.
Ridge, Joseph. 15.34.
Nancy A. 34.
Isaac. 15.
Ridley. George. 21
Robertson, Col. ___ 21.
Charles,16.
22.
Rogers, Russell. 3.
Rockwood, John. 2.
Root, Dr. Thos. 1.
Ross, David. 36.
Ruble, Elizabeth. 3.
Owen. 3.
Russell, George. 19.
Rutherford, Wm. 3.
Saunders, Deshea. 3
Scale, C. B. 19.
Scott, Lot. 16.
Scruggs, Gross. 5.
James. 32.
Margaret. 30.
Sells, Louisa 28
Sevier, Capt. 21
John 16.
Valentine 16.
Shackleford,David D. 26
Sharp, Ensgn Abram.25
Shelton, Minerva Jane
30.
Sherfey.C. 27
E. 27
Shipp, James. 23.
Shipley, Benj. 28.
18.
Capt. 28
Nathan. 21.
Simpson, James. 16
Slaven,Minervia. 29.
Slaughter , Wm. 27

Smith, Ann. 9.
    Bird.B. 9.
    Elizabeth. 9.
    Guy.9.
        7
    Jenny. 9.
    Jennie, E. 18.
    John. 9
    Kate Bowker. 9
    Lucy. 9.
    Nancy. 19
    Sarah. 4.
    Susannah. 9
    Thomas 14.
Smithson, Samuel. 37.
Spurgin. E. 27
Stagg, Mary. 13.
Stearns, John. 19.
Stein, Nathan. 12.
Stewart, James. 19.36.
    John. 11.
    Reuben. 11.
Stephenson,Elizabeth.26
      27.
    Joshua. 20.21
Sutherland, Sally. 3.
Swann, Judith. 1.
Swingle, George. 19
    John. 19.
Talbot, Agnes. 24.
    Charles.5.11.
    Edmund. 7.11.
    Haile. 11.22
    Isham.4.5.
    James. 11.
    John. 9.
    Matt. 5.
    Matthew,4.7.11.
      24.

    Matthew Lewis. 11.
    Thomas Green. 11.
    William. 11.
Tate,James. 37.
Tates, David. 33.
Taylor, James, 16.
    Nathaniel 19.
Temple.Angelina. S. 50.
Terry, Samuel. 37.
Thompson, ____ 38.
Tickens,James. 23.
    John. 23.
Timmons, Mary Jane. 30.
Titsworth, Nancy.34.
    Thomas 34.
Tracy, Timothy. 24.
Trebute, Robert. 35.
Trigg, Ann. 9.
    William. 14.
Tucker, Capt. William. 2.
Turman. Eliz. 3.
Turnbull, Sally. 3.
Vaughn, Alex.11.
    Therwood. 27.
Vier, James. 3.
    Josias. 3.
Vincent. George. 21
    Thomas 36.
Wade, John. 3.
    Susannah. 3.
Wainright, John 10.
Walker, ____ 8.
Wallace, Mary. 26.
Walton. Jesse. 16.
Warner, James. D. 10.
Watts, Threetcut. 8.
White. Wm. S. 30.35.
Whitlock, Elizabeth. 24.
    Elizabeth McCrary,
    18.19.

    J.L. 23.
    J.T. 18
    J.S. 24
    Mary.18
    Will. 18.
Whitman. David. 10
    Elizabeth. 10.
Willards. ____ 22.
Willis, Joseph. 12.
Williams, Jno. B. 2.
    N.A. 37.
Wms, Mary. 2.
Woodcock, Robert. 5.
Woodward. ____ 7.
Wright, Thomas. 9.
Yarbrough, Hannah. 9.
    James. 9.
    Jerem . 9
Yates, Robert. 7.
Yoaksley, Jesse. C. 26.
Young, Robert. 22.

*****************************************************

CPSIA information can be obtained
at www.ICGtesting.com
Printed in the USA
LVHW051544300423
745689LV00012B/1253